ON THE EVE OF
COLONIALISM

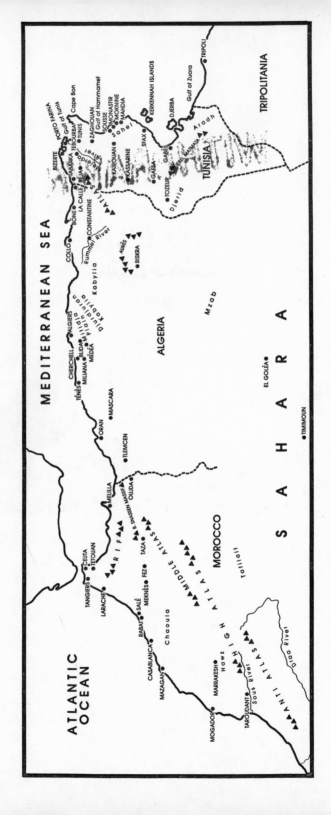

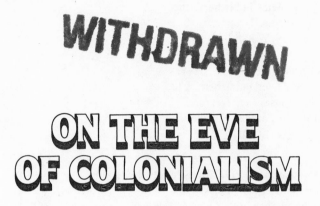

ON THE EVE
OF COLONIALISM

North Africa Before the French Conquest

by Lucette Valensi
Translated by Kenneth J. Perkins

AFRICANA PUBLISHING COMPANY

NEW YORK   LONDON

First published in the United States of America 1977 by
Africana Publishing Company, a division of
Holmes & Meier Publishers, Inc.
101 Fifth Avenue
New York, N.Y. 10003

Great Britain:
Holmes & Meier Publishers, Ltd.
Hillview House
1, Hallswelle Parade, Finchley Road
London, NW11 ODL

English translation ©1977 by Kenneth J. Perkins
©Flammarion et cie., Paris, 1969
Originally published as *Le Maghreb avant la prise d'Alger*
by Flammarion et cie.

LIBRARY OF CONGRESS CATALOGING IN PUBLICATION DATA

Valensi, Lucette.
  On the eve of colonialism
  North Africa Before the French Conquest, 1790-1830.
  Translation of Le Maghreb avant la prise d'Alger, 1790-1830.
  Bibliography: p.
  1. Africa, North — History — 1517-1882. 2. Africa, North — Economic
conditions. 3. Africa, North — Social conditions. I. Title.
DT201.V313   961'.02   77-9589
ISBN 0-8419-0322-0

PRINTED IN THE UNITED STATES OF AMERICA

Contents

Foreword
to The English Edition

Morocco, Algeria, and Tunisia, known collectively in Arabic as the Maghrib — the West — comprise a region which has often been at the periphery of other, larger societies. While linked with the Maghrib in an economic, religious, or political symbiosis, these societies usually paid little attention to the area, viewing it as a world apart from their own. One consequence of this relationship has been a tendency among historians to avoid considering the Maghrib as a socio-political organism in and of itself. This, in turn, has generated confusion about the context in which the Maghrib should properly be studied.

Arab Muslims from the Middle East conquered the Maghrib very early in the era of Islamic expansion, and from North Africa the conquerors, aided by new converts, pushed into Spain, where they fostered a cultural atmosphere brilliantly blending East and West. Nevertheless, the Maghrib, because of its substantial non-Arab (Berber) population which preserved many pre-Islamic traditions, and because of its physical separation from the political and cultural centers of the Middle East, was frequently overlooked in historical studies dealing with the Muslim world.

African historians generally neglect the Maghrib as well, again despite strong evidence that they should not. Islam, a critical religious force south of the Sahara, was introduced from North Africa, and the cities of the southern Mediterranean coast served as outlets for goods coming by caravan from the African interior.

Finally, there is Mediterranean society itself. The Maghrib was often deemed in, but not of, that society, with events of consequence transpiring on the European shores of the Mediterranean. The people of "Barbary" were the "extras", never the stars, in the dramas which unfolded around the inland sea. Perhaps the ultimate expression of the Maghrib's secondary role in the Mediterranean was France's assertion of dominance over Algeria in 1830, Tunisia in 1881, and Morocco in 1912.

France's imperial concerns with North Africa generated many historical, political, sociological, and anthropological studies of the region and gave birth to genuine scholarly interest in the Maghrib. This interest, which continued after independence and which accepted the Maghrib as a legitimate, self-contained area of study, can only be regarded as a positive effect of the generally negative colonial experience. Virtually every significant work done on North Africa during the 19th century and the first half of the 20th, however, came from the pens of Frenchmen, whether academicians or others with direct experience of the North African colonies and protectorates.

A glance at this work's bibliography verifies this assertion. It is important to bear in mind that this is not a question of a bibliography being skewered to the tastes and requirements of a French-speaking audience; it is rather a question of French studies being all that were available. This situation is now in the process of change. As French scholars continue to produce excellent studies on all phases of Maghribi history, they are being joined by others, bringing new perspectives to, and offering new interpretations of, the region's past. Of particular importance in this respect are

North African intellectuals who are now beginning to write their own histories of their countries and make them available in the language of the region, and English-speaking students of the Maghrib, who are compiling a corpus of literature which has opened a door to one of the last areas of the world about which information has been generally lacking for speakers of English.

It is unfortunate, if understandable, that much of the interest of non-French historians has focused on a few aspects of the Maghrib's recent past. The political and economic conditions which permitted and, indeed, encouraged the establishment of European domination have been examined, as have the mechanisms by which that domination was implemented and the indigenous reactions which it aroused. The development of nationalist ideologies and the growth of the countries of North Africa after independence have also been stressed. Such studies are certainly useful and important, and countless more are needed to provide us with a fuller and more accurate understanding of the Maghrib in the 19th and 20th centuries than we have even now.

There can be no doubt that North Africa's co-optation into the orbit of the modern, European world through colonialism was a traumatic and disruptive experience. In studying the area, the onset of colonialism presents a natural watershed — the beginning of a phase during which all previously accepted and cherished notions are subject to dramatic change. The logical starting point for a history of modern North Africa must be 1830. Clearly, however, it is not possible to comprehend the significance of the transformations which occurred (although the transformations themselves may be fairly obvious) without understanding what Maghribi society had been and how it had operated. To argue that colonialism altered essential patterns of life in the Maghrib is pointless, even if true, unless substantial evidence can be produced to illustrate conditions in the precolonial Maghrib. Only then does the impact of colonialism assume realistic proportions, because only then can it be perceived in approximately the same light as it was by those who experienced it. Professor Valensi's book is an excellent step in this direction, and a volume to which English-speaking students of the Maghrib should have access.

Because little on the precolonial Maghrib had been written in or translated into English until recently, gross misconceptions about the region have been perpetuated. One of the most obvious and most persistent of these concerns is the "Barbary pirates." Professor Valensi points out that the practice labelled as "piracy" in western literature was by no means a monopoly of the North Africans. European nations, and even the Knights of Malta, recognizing the existence of a more or less permanent state of war between themselves, as Christians, and the Muslims of the Mediterranean, engaged in similar practices. But there is another misconception about this "piracy" which is even more basic than the assessment of guilt or its more accurate and honest distribution. These undertakings were not piracy at all, but privateering, and the distinction, although apparently semantic at first glance, is much more. The latter term suggests a legitimacy conferred by a state of war; the former suggests banditry and no more. Just as American historians would take exception to calling the privateers of the Civil War era pirates, so also the student of the Maghrib bristles at the continuation of serious misinterpretations in his area.

Another misconception about the Maghrib which abounds and which is linked to the "piracy" issue, is that North Africa was a stronghold of barbarism prior to France's assumption of control, after which civilization slowly trickled in. Such an attitude had its roots in 19th century French propaganda. It comforted the colonizer, and also eased his dealings with both rivals and allies, to aver that without French rule the people of North Africa would be forever doomed to lives of ignorance, backwardness, and poverty. Professor Valensi's descriptions of trade, commerce, and industry indicate that, while the Maghrib suffered through hard times in the late 1700s, neither its people nor its culture were inherently inferior to those of Europe.

It is to be hoped, then, that this volume will enhance the study of modern North Africa in English-speaking environments by illuminating the often overlooked period immediately before colonial control began and correcting misimpressions about it. It can also be useful to students of the Arab East, since it shows what a traditional society elsewhere in the Muslim world was like. The book is of value to students of European history who can profit from observing the workings of a society into which Europe was about to pour vast amounts of money and manpower as it pursued its imperial ambitions. Finally, the work should prove to be an asset, in a comparative context, to students of other parts of the "Third World" which underwent similar experiences, since it can provide some insights about the extent to which precolonial (or traditional or preindustrial) societies shared basic characteristics.

In translating this work, a number of modifications in the original have been made, the most important of which was the updating, by the author, of portions of the text. Other changes have been the work of the translator. Arabic and Berber words, for example, are transliterated slightly differently in French than in English, and it is the latter form which has been employed. French spellings have been retained for geographic terms not commonly seen in English, since the French versions are the more widely accepted ones. Transliteration devices have been kept to a minimum. The symbol ' indicates the Arabic letter *'ain.*

The original version of this book was intended for a readership which had some familiarity with North Africa, and definitions of basic Arabic and Berber terms and explanatory footnotes were not felt to be necessary. In adapting the book for its new audience, notes have been included. Arabic and Berber words marked with an asterisk in the text are defined in the glossary.

K.J.P.

Preface

On July 5, 1830, Algiers, "the bulwark of the Holy War," fell into the hands of France. Tunisia and Morocco escaped this fate for a time, but in turn, they too succumbed to French tutelage. Although the military confrontation was short-lived, the conflict between the two cultures continued until independence was again secured. An understanding of this clash requires a knowledge of the Maghrib before the conquest — its society, its economy, and its peoples' spiritual values. Jacques Berque has reminded us of this:

"In North Africa," he wrote in *Dépossession du monde*, "the violence of the liberation struggle nourished a bitter, sometimes frenzied, literature denouncing the wounds inflicted by colonialism. In short, the literature retained from the colonial dialectic only the outer layer, and of that only what was destructive. This deficiency in analysis omits what undoubtedly was most important statistically and logically: the permanence or intrinsic mutation of the inviolate."

There is something more. After seizing technologically backward regions, France left them underdeveloped. In place of a long-standing equilibrium — which, it must be added, stemmed from inertia — were substituted serious

disequilibriums, upsetting the operation of Maghribi
societies and making economic growth a categorical imperative. Among the conditions which influenced, accelerated,
or restrained the process of "take off" were some legacies of
the past. As deep as the trauma of conquest and colonialism
may have been, and as destructive as their effects on some
segments of North African life were, some old structures did
resist, were reformed, and functioned, in spite of changes.
These forms, eroded but still discernible, can never be
ignored in any model for development. This work attempts
to show them in their precolonial pattern.

Chronology

Morocco

1790-1792	Moulay Yazid sultan
1792-1822	Moulay Slimane sultan
1792-1796	Defeat of a number of pretenders to the throne
1811	Beginning of a period of bloody disorders
1819-1822	Upheaval throughout the empire
1822-1859	Moulay 'Abd al-Rahman sultan

Algeria

July 12, 1791	Death of Muhammad Dey. Accession of Baba Hassan
1792	Evacuation of Oran by the Spanish. Treaty with Spain
May 14, 1798	Accession of Mustafa

1799	Algiers and Tunis break relations with France
1800	Peace with France
1801	Another break in relations and the reestablishment of peace
1805	Famine. Massacre of the Jews
August 30, 1805	Mustafa assassinated. Ahmad proclaimed dey
1807	Conflict between Tunis and Algiers
November 7, 1808	Ahmad beheaded. 'Ali al-Rassal proclaimed dey
February 7, 1809	'Ali al-Rassal strangled. Hajj 'Ali proclaimed dey
July, 1813	Siege of Le Kef by the armed forces of Constantine, ending in a Tunisian victory. Revolt in Oran.
1814-1815	Revolt in Kabylia
March 22, 1815	Hajj 'Ali strangled. Muhammad Khaznadji proclaimed dey
April 7, 1815	Muhammad Khaznadji strangled. 'Umar Agha proclaimed dey
July 7, 1815	Treaty with the United States
1816	Lord Exmouth's naval demonstration
October 8, 1816	'Umar Dey strangled. 'Ali Khodja becomes dey
1821	Reestablishment of peace between Algiers and Tunis
1824	Revolt in Kabylia
April 30, 1827	The "coup d'éventail"

June 15, 1827	Beginning of French blockade of Algiers
May 11, 1830	Embarcation of French troops for Algiers
July 5, 1830	Capture of Algiers

Tunisia

1782	Accession of Hammuda Pasha
1790	Peace with Spain
1793	Victorious war against Tripoli
1802	Peace with France
1811	Revolt and dissolution of the militia
September 15, 1814	Death of Hammuda Pasha. Accession of 'Uthman
December 21, 1814	'Uthman assassinated. Accession of Mahmud
March 28, 1824	Death of Mahmud. Accession of Hussain Bey
August 8, 1830	New treaty with France

Introduction:
Africa Ignored

One of the best ways to become acquainted with precolonial North Africa would be to take an exploratory voyage there, using the writings of 18th century men who frequented its coasts and left accounts of their adventures or descriptions of the countries they visited. The dearth of material on the three countries of the Maghrib is, however, distressing.

The Maghrib as Seen from Europe

One measure of this inadequacy is quantitative. We know, at least for the French publishing business, what place geography or descriptions of manners and customs occupied in the printed material of the 18th century. The lists of publication permits[1] assigned to authors and booksellers in the second half of the century provide revealing figures. Several hundred volumes obtained the privilege of publication. Among them, religious writing, medical literature, grammar, and music were predominant, while geography was a secondary topic. At the end of the Ancien Régime, treatises on seemingly more practical matters such as agriculture, economics, politics, and the mathematical sciences replaced liturgical and devotional books. Geographical and ethnographic literature remained inconsequential. Although a certain taste for the exotic did emerge, North Africa was not "wild" enough to merit attention.

Similar research on the production and distribution of English language books has not yet been executed. Nevertheless, in English as in French, the vogue for large historical and geographical series was quite extensive, and the number of their editions indicates the curiosity of the reading public of the time. What did they say about the Maghrib?

In Moreri's *Grand dictionnaire historique* (1749), the articles on Morocco, Algeria, and Tunisia were uncritical and unrevised compilations of earlier writings by Marmol, Leo Africanus, Mouette, or Laugier de Tassy.[2] As a result, the populations of cities were immutably fixed from century to century, edition to edition. The *Grand dictionnaire géographique et critique* of Bruzen de la Martinière (1768), reprinted several times in the 18th century, fell into the same category. Summary descriptions of the capital cities and governments were all these compilations offered. At least they were not judgmental. Later works, including Jacques Grasset de Saint-Sauveur's *Encyclopédie des voyages* (1796), were more subjective and did not hesitate to include value judgments. This volume's typical image of late 18th-century North Africans emphasized first the vice of lust.

> The Turks and Algerians, not anxious for large families, behave as true pirates on the marital bed. They ravage the fields of sensual delight without making any effort to have them bear fruit. The women, resigned to their fate, suffer further insults since almost none of these petty sultans, taking Jupiter of Greek mythology as a model, hesitate to abandon Hebe for Ganymede.

A second vice was laziness.

> Nature fertilizes their lands in vain; the slothful citizens turn deaf ears to the imprecations of nature.

Moreover,

> Superstition and despotism will shortly have transformed
> this breeding ground of fine men into a desert. The Qur'an
> and the cudgel do not suffice to make heads of families happy
> in a promising, but poorly cultivated, region.

To the author, all these defects justified his final query:

> When will those nations concerned about the freedom of the
> seas unite in a political crusade against this African rabble
> whose brigandage is encouraged only by our patience?

The literature, then, focused on ethics rather than on ethnology. In describing North African "customs," the writers assigned the society a set of frequently negative attributes which were wholly inadequate to explain it, and which left their readers still unaware of reality.

Travellers, however, had a better feel for the countries, and some collected their impressions and observations in order to publish memoirs. More often than not, though, their manuscripts were rescued from oblivion only in the 19th and 20th centuries. Dr. Peyssonel made a voyage to Algeria and Tunisia in 1724-1725 and Desfontaines, also a doctor, went in 1784-1785. Yet the accounts of their trips were not published until 1838.[3] The picture of the Regency of Tunis drawn by Dr. Frank, who visited the country on two occasions early in the 19th century, was printed only in 1850.[4] Not until 1898 did *Alger au XVIII ème siècle* by Venture de Paradis reach the public, and Poiron's *Mémoires concernant l'état présent du Royaume de Tunis,* dating from 1752, did not appear until 1925. In spite of the fact that Abbé Raynal wrote one of the greatest publishing successes of the 18th century, the famous *Histoire philosophique et politique des établissements et du commerce européen dans les deux Indes,* his *Mémoire sur Tunis* remained unpublished until 1948.

On the other hand, some works were well received, becoming objects of translations, forgeries, and multiple editions. There were French, English, and Italian versions of the *Histoire des états barbaresques qui exercent la piraterie* by Laugier de Tassy (1757), while the same author's *Histoire du Royaume d'Alger*, first published in 1725, reappeared with a new title in 1737 and was counterfeited by Le Roy in 1750. Thomas Shaw's *Travels and Observations Relating to Several Parts of Barbary and Levant* (1738) soon had French, German, and Dutch translations. Similarly, Lemprière's *A Tour from Gibraltar to Tangier, Sallee, Mogadore, and Santa Cruz* (1791) experienced several editions and translations. Nevertheless, the work of Thomas Pellow best stood the test of time. A century and a half after the original publication, it was reprinted in a popular collection of adventure tales. Its highly descriptive title is enough to explain its success: *The History of the Long Captivity and Adventures of Thomas Pellow in South Barbary, Giving an Account of His Being Taken by Sallee Rovers and Carryed as a Slave to Mequinez at Eleven of Age; His Various Adventures in That Country for the Space of Twenty Years, Escape, and Return Home; With an Account of the Manners and Customs of the Moors, the Cruelty of Their Emperors, a Relation of the Wars which Happened in the Kingdoms of Fez and Morocco from 1720 to 1736, a Description of the Cities and Buildings, Miseries of Christian Slaves, and Other Curiosities.*

In what may be termed the "Barbary Cycle," the topics occupying the most attention were clearly privateering and Christian slavery. In France, England, and Italy countless adventure tales, reports on negotiations to ransom captives, and lists of freed slaves or "orders of procession," which also advertised the redemption orders,[5] appeared. Although these writings died out in England in the mid-18th century, the themes of ransom and privateering continued in France and Italy until the end of the Napoleonic Wars. At that point, the restitution of peace in Europe provided a final theme — the elimination of the corsairs by the collective action of the Christian powers.

From Stereotype to Objective View

There were still other contemporary witnesses, including European consuls living in Tunis, Algiers, and Tangiers, and slaves. The latter, in direct contact with their masters, were undoubtedly more familiar with Maghribi society. Fortunately, some of them, such as Father Caronni, a slave in Tunis, or the writer Pananti, a captive in Algiers, left journals of their experiences.[6] The consuls, who lived in the country for a long time and corresponded with their superiors regularly, albeit slowly because of transportation and communication facilities, might also be expected to provide copious answers for questions which must be posed. However, they were restricted to the cities in which they lived, travelled only rarely, and were preoccupied with their duties, which included protecting the interests of their king, assisting merchants from their homeland, and aiding European slaves. Thus they had little time to concern themselves with life in the country as a whole, and even in the cities, Muslim society remained closed to them. Since few of them spoke Arabic, they could communicate with the North Africans only in the *lingua franca*, a mixture of broken Arabic, French, Italian, and Spanish or, more normally, by utilizing one of the almost obligatory intermediaries between Muslims and Europeans, a Jewish interpreter. They were never permitted to enter the homes of the city. If a revolt or palace coup erupted, they filed a report on it, but they were as uninformed about day-to-day urban life as they were about the peasantry. Morocco remained especially incomprehensible, for as late as 1835 there were no Christians in its three capitals or the provinces. Only foreign ambassadors could travel in the interior to meet the sovereign, although even then they could do so only under escort. They could not spend the night in cities or villages, but had to camp outside. Nor could they directly enter the city where the sultan* had consented to receive them, but instead entered the Jewish quarter where lodgings had been prepared for them. There they waited several days before being summoned to an audience with the ruler. After a brief conversation with him outside the palace, they were permitted to stroll in the gardens, after which they were required to return to Tangiers as they had come.

In any event, why should the consuls not have shared the same prejudices as their contemporaries? Whether in consular reports or in travel literature, the reader learns more about the values of 18th-century writers than about what they observed. Bearing this in mind, it is possible to distinguish three broad trends of thought among the authors. The first may be termed "Christian," although in truth it is rather manichaean. People who felt this way viewed the North Africans as incarnations of evil. The stories about ransoming captives best typified this moralistic literature, although traces of it appeared in secular authors as well. Saint Gervais, for example, accused the Moors of such base sentiments as cheating, greed, sloth, intemperance, gluttony, ingratitude, immoderate love of women, fanaticism against the Christians, and many more.[7]

It was this trend which fueled fictional literature. Captivity, rape, forced conversion, the search for a loved one carried into slavery, and escape, were all adventures in which the Turk (a term used indiscriminantly for any Muslim of the Mediterranean Basin) was the villain, and the Christian either the virtuous victim or the hero. To catch a glimpse of this, one need only recall Voltaire's "Story of the Old Woman" or his tearful Zaire; the fate of Rossini's *Italian in Algiers,* or the opera's comic parody *Il Pampaluco con Cassandro Taddeo Kaimakan* by Teoli, in which it is said the use of the pike is as common as the use of coffee in Algiers. Similarly, in Neapolitan folklore, the echoes of the corsair experience embodied stereotypes of North Africans, whether Turks or Moors, which were of a nature to provoke frightful terror in the Christian consciousness. These attitudes stemmed from incursions which Italy's coastal populations endured as late as the 18th century, but for others, who no longer needed to fear the corsairs' raids, they were products of their imaginations, which remained faithful to old literary themes. It is tempting to paraphrase Carl Jung: It was the sneering face of his own evil "shadow" which western man recognized on the other shore of the Mediterranean.

There were, however, wise and magnanimous literary sultans, in *Zaire* or the *Abduction from the Seraglio,* for example. The travellers Peyssonel and Desfontaines exemplified this second "philosophical" trend which was less ethnocentric and even somewhat apologetic. As has been noted, however, their works were unknown in the 18th century. Abbé Poiret, suffused with the spirit of the Enlightenment, discovered in North Africa the superiority of the state of nature to that of the more refined countries. He traced Muslim hatred of Christians to the Crusades and to Christian fanaticism. Nevertheless, the author often contradicted himself by relating highly improbable tales about the cruelty, greed, and superstition of the Arabs. Less wordy, Abbé Raynal provided a description of conditions in Tunis without fantasizing. The wisdom of its government, the diligence of its inhabitants, and the variety of its products all characterized a civilized country which, on balance, hardly differed from the Christian nations.

The third trend was political, revolving consciously, and ever more frequently, around the concept of a commercial or territorial conquest of North Africa.[8] Although expansionist in their conclusions, such works contained an abundance of more precise facts. Indeed, during the first third of the 19th century, with MacGill, Frank, and Jackson, writings based on careful observation became more common, providing a more reliable base of information about the Maghrib. After the conquest of Algiers, both the quality and quantity of documentation expanded as the area of investigation broadened and the frontiers of the known world were pushed back to the desert.

Regardless of the trends into which specific works fall — and there is no detectable chronological pattern — it is imperative to review all contemporary works with great scrutiny to separate credible facts from clichés and fiction.

The Silence of the North Africans

For a long time, then, the North Africans were simply infidels and barbarians misusing a prodigiously fertile soil. But ethnocentrism was a widely shared characteristic, and at the same time, the Muslims saw the Christians as infidels, equally despicable and unfamiliar.

The three Maghribi states did not maintain merchant fleets which could have put them in direct contact with European ports. The maritime wars of the Napoleonic period provided North African vessels the opportunity to enter Europe, but at the time the possibility was minimally exploited and was not pursued afterwards. No North African merchants or consuls lived in Europe except for a few Jewish subjects of the Moroccan sultan, one of whom acted as a consul, at Gibraltar and Cadiz, and no Muslim travelled on the northern shore of the Mediterranean. Only the privateers and the slaves were familiar with the Christian world. In brief, the two cultures were ignorant of each other.

Did the North Africans at least provide information about themselves? Not at all. It was as if an intellectual paralysis had stricken the Maghrib, and yet in all three countries an intense cultural life flourished. Moulay Slimane, the Moroccan sovereign, was a studious, reflective man and a strict observer of his religious duties. Most Muslims received some training in reading and writing. The rapid spread of the Rahmaniyya and Tijaniyya Brotherhoods in the late 18th and early 19th centuries demonstrated the milieu's receptivity to the teachings of the savants who founded these orders. Intellectual progress was, however, gravely retarded because religious writings, especially sterile Qur'anic commentaries and exegeses, or biographies of saints, remained its focal point. Only a handful of chroniclers deviated from the rule: al-Zayyani in Morocco; al-Hajj Ahmad al-Mubarak in the beylik of Constantine; Maqdish al-Sfaxi, Hammuda ibn 'Abd al-Aziz, Baji al-Mas'udi, and Saghir ibn Yusuf in Tunisia.[9] None of these writers bears favorable comparison with medieval Islamic thinkers. The 18th-century Maghrib certainly produced no Ibn Khalduns.[10]

To make matters worse, printing was still unknown in all three countries. If a new concept arose, it could be transmitted only by word of mouth or in longhand. Even today, not all the chronicles cited have been printed and many remain poorly known. Agreements between individuals or groups were also oral, for memory merited more credence than the written word. Finally, administrative documents were more often destroyed than preserved.

The Maghrib of the "obscure centuries" thus remains opaque.[11] At best, its political history and the vicissitudes of its relations with the countries of Christian Europe — in a word, the events — are known. But what of the areas beyond these superficial events — what is known of the peasants or the artisans, their numbers, social organization, or material life, their beliefs or aspirations? Such important information is elusive. It is possible to learn about such matters only by associating the bits and pieces of information gleaned from the past — from Moroccan and Tunisian archives supplemented by Italian, French, and English consular materials — with other information which the present, or the recent past, provides. From this period, better known because colonial rule encouraged tireless investigation by French analysts, it is possible to begin to move backwards towards an understanding of the older society.

Notes

1. During the Ancien Régime in France, the publishing business was controlled by the royal administration in order to (1) guarantee the monopoly of booksellers by the grant of a "privilege," and (2) to block the publication of books hostile to the religion or the state. See François Furet et al., *Livre et société dans la France du XVIIIe siècle.* (Paris and The Hague, 1965 and 1970).

2. Luis del Marmol-Carvajal, *Descripción general de Africa*, 3 vols. (Granada and Malaga, 1573-1599); Germain Mouette, *Histoire des conquêtes de Mouley Archy connu sous le nom de roy de Tafilet, et de Mouley Ismael* (Paris, 1683); Laugier de Tassy, *Histoire des états barbaresques qui exercent la piraterie* (Paris, 1757); Laugier de Tassy, *Histoire du royaume d'Alger avec l'état présent de son gouvernement* (Amsterdam, 1725); and Leo Africanus, *Description de l'Afrique, tierce partie du monde* (Lyons, 1556).

3. Jean-André Peyssonel and Louis-René Desfontaines, *Voyages dans les régences de Tunis et d'Alger*, 2 vols. (Paris, 1838).

4. Louis Frank, *Tunis, description de cette régence* (Paris, 1850).

5. The redemption orders were Catholic religious groups which devoted themselves to the ransoming of slaves, as well as tending to their spiritual and material needs while in captivity in the Maghrib. The "orders of procession" were pamphlets laying out an order of march for freed slaves who were paraded through the European ports on their return from imprisonment.

6. Felice Caronni, *Voyage chez les barbaresques* (Paris, 1805); and Filippo Pananti, *Avventure e osservazioni di Filippo Pananti sopra le coste di Barberia*, 3 vols. (Milan, 1817).

7. Saint-Gervais, *Mémoires historiques qui concernent le gouvernement de l'ancien et du nouveau royaume de Tunis* (Paris, 1736), pp. 170-71.

8. See, for example, Thomas MacGill, *Account of Tunis* (London, 1811); Domingo Badia y Leblich (Ali Bey al-Abbassi), *The Travels of Ali Bey*, 2 vols. (Philadelphia, 1816); and James Grey Jackson, *An Account of the Empire of Morocco and the Districts of Sus and Tafilelt* (London, 1809).

9. Abu al-Qasim ibn Ahmad al-Zayyani, *al-Turjuman al-mu 'rib 'an duwal al-mashriq wa 'l-maghrib* (in French translation as *Le Maroc de 1631 à 1812* (Paris, 1886); A. Dournon, "Kitab tarikh Qosantîna, par el Hadj Ahmed El Mobârek," *Revue Africaine*, no. 289, 1913, pp. 265-306; Maqdish al-Sfaxi, *Nuzhat al-anzar fi al-'aja'ib at-tawarikh wa 'l-akhbar*, parts of which are translated in C.A. Nallino, *Venezia e Sfax nel secolo XVIII secondo il cronista arabo Maqdish*, *Centenario della nascita di Michele Amari*, vol. 1, pp. 306-356 (Palermo, 1910); Hammuda ibn 'Abd al-Aziz, *Kitab al-Basha;* Muhammad Baji al-Mas 'udi, *al-Khulasah an-naqiyyah fi umara' Ifriqiyyah;* and V. Serres and Mohammed Lasram, *Mechra el-Melki, chronique tunisienne, 1705-1771* (Paris, 1900), a French version of *Mashru' al-milki*.

10. Ibn Khaldun (1332-1406) spent a considerable portion of his adult life in North Africa holding various government offices and writing a history of the Berbers. He is recognized as a father of sociology and as one of the most original thinkers of the Islamic medieval era.

11. The phrase "obscure centuries" comes from the subtitle of a work

by Emile Gautier, *Le Passé de l'Afrique du nord*, first issued in 1937 as *L'Islamisation de l'Afrique du nord*. The work deals with a much earlier period, but the reference to the obscurity of the Maghrib's history is apt.

ON THE EVE OF
COLONIALISM

1.
A Thinly Populated Land

The first important fact about North African society was the dispersal of a sparse population over an immense area. The Maghrib's population early in the 19th century was significantly smaller than it is today. Tunisia had just over a million inhabitants; some three million people, according to the most reliable calculations, lived in Algeria in 1830; and contemporary estimates placed the number of Moroccans between five and fifteen million. Overall, the population was roughly a third of what it is at present.

Irruptions of Disease

More significant than absolute numbers are demographic trends. Disease sapped the Maghrib of much of its strength, not only because of a lack of sanitary conditions or doctors — on the whole, most rural societies of the time were equally deprived — but especially because of repeated epidemics of fatal illnesses which made North Africa, at the end of the 18th and the beginning of the 19th century, a region of endemic disease. The plague, generally carried by pilgrims coming from Alexandria, constantly afflicted the Maghrib, breaking out first in the port cities and later spreading to the countryside where it was extremely destructive.

This scourge first appeared in 1784, striking Tunisia and then Algeria, but sparing Morocco. The plague ravaged the interior of both regencies, as well as the coasts. Although it subsided in Tunisia in 1785, the disease continued in Algeria, where it flared up with increased virulence in the east during 1787, in the center of the country the next year, and in Mascara in 1789, finally reaching Tlemcen in 1790-91. Tunisia, which had not experienced an epidemic since 1705, lost from one-third to one-sixth of its population. Many members of the Tunis guilds of wool weavers, chechia* manufacturers, and mat makers perished, and the latter group was left with only one master craftsman in 1786. There were similar economic effects in Algeria where the quantity of wool which the Africa Company[1] exported from Bône doubled in 1787 because of the insufficient number of burnous* weavers to process the wool gathered. Algiers' silk industry also suffered a reduction in the production and export of its goods.

After only a brief respite, the plague reappeared in 1793. Although less acute, this attack proved equally dangerous, for the disease struck the same places several times, diminishing only to recur. Even Morocco, which had avoided contamination since 1752, was affected by the disease, which entered the country from Algeria in 1799. Famine had increased the empire's susceptibility to infection and the constant expeditions of the Sharifian army hastened the propagation of the plague. It spread to Fez, Meknes, Rabat, and the Hawaz, ravaging the country from Tangiers to the Sous Valley. In 1800 the southern reaches of the country shook off the pestilence, but it continued unabated in the north and east. Algeria endured the disease from 1793 until 1799, and even longer in its western regions. The Tunisian Sahel*, in the meanwhile, remained healthy, although plague conditions prevailed in Tunis every year from 1794 to 1800 except for 1799.

A third onslaught came in 1817. Algeria was the first victim, opening the door for the epidemic's further expansion. Shortly afterwards, pilgrim ships brought the plague to Tangiers, in June, and to Tunis, late in August, 1818. The epidemic lasted almost two years in each country, again spreading through the cities and the countryside. Famine preceded and accompanied the outbreaks and an epizootic disease decimated the cattle. In Tunisia, a quarter of the population died. An observer in Bône noted that in October, 1818, two-thirds of the city's houses were boarded up, indicating the terrible destructiveness of the plague. Even this, however, did not exhaust it, since it recurred in Algeria in a lesser form until 1822. After this lapse, North Africa never again fell prey to a serious attack of bubonic plague.

Pilgrimage routes were highways of contagion, as André Siegfried has already demonstrated.[2] Improvements in transportation gradually increased the threat of contagion. The cholera pandemic of 1827-37 bypassed Tunisia but reached Algeria in 1834 and Morocco in 1835.

Totally without medical aid, the rural population could offer no resistance to these attacks short of seeking safety in flight. In the major cities, an awareness of preventive measures practiced in Europe left the Muslims torn between submission to the divine will and their instinct to survive.

During the 1818 epidemic, wrote the Tunisian chronicler Bin Diyaf,[3] a controversy split the population. Advocates of quarantine procedures based their position on Muhammad's advice to "flee the leper as the lion," while others argued that nothing could avert fate. Because of the close links between medicine and religion, two Islamic scholars holding contradictory opinions published elaborate dissertations based on canonical texts. The policies adopted by the rulers reflected these questions of conscience, sometimes resulting in the imposition of quarantine or the creation of *cordons sanitaires* around the infected regions (in Tunis in 1786), but at other times ending in a reliance on fate and a refusal to break external contacts (in Morocco in 1799). Years later, in

June, 1818, the sultan yielded to the pressure of the European consuls and fixed the duration and the site for the quarantine of pilgrims arriving from Alexandria. Nevertheless, he ordered the governor of Tangiers to allow passengers to land at once, and within a few days the plague broke out in the city. There were no doctors to make a positive diagnosis, but its presence was unmistakable.

Once any disease gained a foothold, there were no effective means of fighting it. Emetics, blood-letting, and the use of pungent plant vapors were the only known "remedies." To make matters worse, indiscriminate mingling often subjected healthy individuals to contact with the sick and sometimes even with the dead. In Morocco, during the 1818 epidemic, the sultan ordered a new treatment based on drinking, and anointing the body with, olive oil. Its effect was to weaken the parasites — a beneficial, if accidental, result, since their part in the transmission of the illness was totally unknown. The Moroccan Jews followed these instructions and appear to have resisted contamination well. In Tunis, on the other hand, the Jews, along with the lower classes, were particularly hard hit, over 900 perishing in Tunis alone from September, 1818, until May 7, 1819, during an epidemic which lingered for another fifteen months.

Agrarian Calamities

To the misfortunes occasioned by the plague, whose chronology and geographical extent alone can be analyzed since accurate mortality statistics have never been compiled, must be added the dangers of two other diseases: smallpox, which affected the younger population but whose pattern of recurrence is unclear, and the potentially fatal fevers at the end of the summer, which were common from Tunisia to Morocco. On top of all of these, adverse weather conditions sometimes led to shortages and famines.

It is impossible to reconstruct the fluctuations of the harvest across North Africa since the data simply do not exist. It suffices to note only the calamities — shortages which forced starving peasants to migrate or resulted in urban rioting and deaths. The crises did not always occur simultaneously throughout the area. In Morocco, the harvests failed in 1798 and 1799; in Tunisia, the shortages of the winter of 1804 turned to famine after the next summer's poor harvest; and in 1805 Algeria lacked sufficient grain. Prices spiralled in the cities, and the prospect of starvation caused a revolt in Constantine province; Morocco, however, was able to supply its own needs.

After 1815, the western Maghrib again endured hard times. In June, 1816, it was noted that "the year which has just ended was extremely bad for every crop harvested. Locusts devastated the richest grain-producing regions so extensively that quantities which would ordinarily sell for a franc and a quarter have been costing six or seven francs for the past six months."[4] The harvests of 1816, 1817, and 1818 were no better, and Morocco had to import food from Gibraltar — an exceptional turn of events.

In Algeria, locusts damaged the 1815 harvest, and wheat was everywhere in short supply. The dey* forbade its export from Oran or Constantine and even imported some to provision the capital. State storehouses were also opened in an unsuccessful attempt to avert unrest, and serious shortages continued in 1816.

Shortfalls of the same magnitude were avoided in Tunisia, although it experienced a mediocre harvest in each year from 1815 to 1817. Normally a grain exporter, Tunisia appealed to Naples and Alexandria for more wheat. Prices remained high in 1818, exports of grain being forbidden, and in 1820 the regency again imported grain from the Levant when a drought curtailed the harvest and both famine and plague were rampant.

Insufficiencies recurred in Morocco in 1822, 1824, and 1825. In the fall of 1825, peasants demanding food poured into Tangiers and that winter starvation claimed lives both in the major cities of Fez, Meknes, and Rabat, and among the tribes. The ports of Tangiers and Tetouan forestalled disaster by importing wheat, but in the spring a deadly fever broke out. It found countless victims among the undernourished population whose condition had so deteriorated that many people were eating the carcasses of animals which had died from epizootic diseases.

Yet 1824 and 1825 were especially abundant years in Tunis. Subsequent harvests of both grain and olives, which the farmers of the Sahel had sold in advance to European merchants, were, however, poor or nonexistent.

Throughout North Africa, then, a succession of bad harvests doomed the inhabitants to long periods of malnutrition. Moreover, the infrequency of ample harvests prevented the accumulation of adequate reserves, while repeated epidemics and famines added their own adverse effects.

Can these effects be measured? In comparison with Europe, North Africa's demography most closely resembled that of the Ancien Régime in France as described by Pierre Goubert.[5] In both societies, the timing and regularity of crises insured that the renewal of the population could be achieved only by a very high birth rate. It is questionable whether the population of the Maghrib was capable of growing at all. Xavier Yacono for example, has proven that Algeria's population declined between 1830 and 1872,[6] and while problems stemming from the French occupation undoubtedly contributed to this regression, they were certainly not its sole cause. Moreover, Morocco, as yet uncolonized, also underwent a period of continuous turmoil which affected it numerically. Quite possibly, the onset of demographic decline in North Africa should be dated earlier, at the end of the 18th century. A lack of concrete data prevents the testing of this hypothesis. The only certainty is that the Maghrib in the early 19th century was not burdened by the problem of rapid population growth which now characterizes it, as it does most of the underdeveloped world.

At precisely this same time, however, western Europe was enjoying an incontestable, if irregular, population surge, which underscores the disparity between the two regions. In North Africa this growth spurt came only much later.

The effects of this depression on the society are readily apparent. Man, the producer and consumer, remained scarce — a condition unfavorable for the stimulation of economic activity.

"Africa Divides"

The small size of the population was emphasized by its extreme fragmentation. The Maghrib could boast seven ethnic groups, four Muslim religious rites, and a host of languages and life styles. Such diversity illustrated the axiom of the Caliph 'Umar, who is said to have remarked. "Africa divides."[7]

By the close of the 18th century, however, much time had passed since the waves of invasion from Europe and the Middle East had broken on North Africa. These great migrations were followed by population shifts within the Maghrib, such as the descent of mountain tribes to the plains, movements to the coast from the desert, and the continual import of Turks. In 18th and 19th century Morocco, the migrations of the Sanhadja Berbers modified the tribal structure in the northern part of the country; in Tunisia and Algeria, similar movements made the northern parts of the countries in general and the cities of the coastal plain in particular, places of considerable intermingling, heterogeneity, and social disintegration. These movements did not, however, alter the settlement pattern of the Maghrib's population.

The various elements of the population did have contact with each other, but the North Africans viewed themselves in terms of broad ethnic categories coexisting within a hierarchy.

In Algeria and Tunisia, the Turks stood at the summit. They dwelt in the cities, symbolized the theoretical suzerainty of the Ottoman Empire over the regencies, and constituted their militias. Thus, they were clustered in garrison cities, although military service, as will be seen, was not their only activity. In fact, the bey* of Tunis dissolved the militia after a revolt in 1811. In Algiers, the yearly importation of recruits continued until the French conquest, as did the Turks' ability to install or unseat the dey and to dominate the people. Born in the Levant, the Turks differed from the native majority both by their language and their adhesion to Islam's Hanafite rite. Their numbers were quite small, never exceeding 10,000 men in both countries. The Couloughlis, offspring of marriages between Turks and North African women, were much more numerous, but shared neither the prestige nor the duties of the full-blooded Turks.

The Andalusians, descendants of Moors exiled from Spain, saw themselves, and were generally acknowledged to be, more aristocratic and refined than native Muslims. Morocco, because of its proximity to the Iberian Peninsula, had sheltered them, but many continued on to Algeria or Tunisia where they lived in a dozen villages of their own, strung out in the north of the country and identifiable by their round tile roofs. They were arboriculturists in rural areas and artisans or lawyers in the cities, where they breathed new life into craft industries from Fez to Algiers and Tunis.

Sub-Saharan Africa furnished a fourth group, the Blacks. In Morocco, these " 'abid"* performed the functions of the Turks in the neighboring regencies. Moulay Isma-'il had established a corps of black soldiers by purchasing all the slaves of his kingdom, recruiting Sudanese warriors, and arranging for young Black women to bear future soldiers whom the state would then train. This corps of emancipated slaves, able to survive only by the sultan's largesse, depended entirely on the dynasty, whose interests it dutifully served against the population.[8] Somewhat weakened under Isma 'il's successors, the unit continued to resolve disputes between claimants to the throne and in 1808 still consisted of a sizeable 18,000 men. In addition to their use in this professional army, Blacks, brought to the markets of all three countries by trans-Saharan caravans, also served as household slaves.

At the bottom of the social scale were the Jews, "dogs without a flag," who were despised in all three countries but received worse treatment in Morocco than in Algeria or Tunisia. Unable to own land, they were concentrated in the cities, although in Tunisia, in a pattern discernible before the 18th century, some Jews lived in the deep south, near Djebel Matmata, in the oases of Gabès and Gafsa, and on the island of Djerba. However, some fifteen thousand of the regency's twenty thousand Jews in the early 19th century lived in Tunis. In Morocco, too, although primarily townsmen, many Jews resided in villages only nominally under the control of the central government in a geographical pattern recorded in the 16th century by Leo Africanus and observed again in the 19th with virtually no modification by Charles de Foucauld.[9] Their distribution in Algeria had the same characteristics of low density in the countryside and high concentration in the cities.

The Jews were permitted to practice their faith, but lived under a series of degrading restrictions. Throughout the Maghrib, they lived in separate neighborhoods, were obliged to wear special clothing, and could neither bear arms nor own a mount. They spoke Arabic, but wrote it in Hebrew characters, since the Qur'an was in Arabic script. In Morocco, they had to remove their shoes in Muslim quarters, especially around mosques. Civil unrest invariably incited the pillaging of the Jewish quarter by rioters, whether in Rabat, Marrakesh, Fez, or Algiers. Only Tunis was an exception. Plundered by the Algerians in 1756, the Jewish quarter never again suffered such violation.[10]

Of course, the status of all Jews was not the same. Most of them pursued small businesses, but a few managed to place themselves in the entourage of sovereigns or governors. The Jewish community was composed of two groups: the native, unsophisticated North Africans and the Jewish refugees from the Iberian Peninsula or emigrants from Livorno. The latter, trading with other Mediterranean ports and in contact with European civilization, despised the former and had little to do with them. In Tunisia, their legal status was equivocal. Considering themselves Tuscan citizens, they were delighted to win French protection and sport the *tricolore* cockade during the Empire. In the bey's opinion, however, the only Europeans were the Christians. In 1809 a Tuscan Jew was bastinadoed at the bey's order for daring to call himself a Frenchman. He forced the Jews to remove their cockades and threatened any who claimed French protection with death. Similar incidents occurred when Tunisian Jews adopted European fashions a few years later. In Algiers, the "Livornians," actually an amalgam of Jews from Iberia and Italy, had greater freedom than their local coreligionists, and were both more familiar with the changes occurring in Europe and more prepared to adapt to them. In 1816, the sultan of Morocco took steps echoing those of Hammuda Pasha* in Tunis, ordering the expulsion of European Jews who refused to recognize the restrictions imposed on Moroccan Jews. Many who were unwilling to submit to these degrading customs did flee to Gibraltar or Spain.

These attitudes within the Jewish community attest to a North African awareness of the changes transpiring in Europe, but it is important to remember that no more than a handful of individuals shared these feelings.

In addition to the Turks, Couloughlis, Andalusians, Jews, and Blacks, there were also the infidels, if not in Morocco where there were few Christians outside the Spanish *presidios* of Ceuta and Melilla, at least in Algiers and Tunis. Slaves and renegades, some of whom held high positions in the state, as well as merchants and consuls, constituted a population of several hundred Europeans. Moreover, the prohibition of Muslim privateering terminated the state of war between the regencies and the European Mediterranean powers, encouraging a stream of migration bringing Maltese and Italian islanders, driven by poverty or political repression, to the Maghrib.

It would, however, be misleading to conclude that there

was general fragmentation in Maghribi society, since the groups noted accounted for only a few thousand people, while the Arabs and Berbers were numbered in millions. The Maghrib's ethnic composition was considerably simplified outside the cities. Berbers and Arabs had a common heritage, although language and, as will be seen, culture kept them apart. In Tunisia there were almost no Berbers, but in Algeria they lived in Kabylia, the Aurès Mountains, and the Sahara, comprising some 50 percent of the population. Berbers were in the majority in Morocco before the protectorate, with the Rif, the Beni Snassen Massif, the Middle Atlas, High Atlas, and Anti-Atlas, the Sous Valley, and the Tafilalt, all predominantly Berber regions.

To learn what structural elements underlay this ethnic, religious, and linguistic diversity, we must turn from the often misleading cities and examine the countryside.

Notes

1. The Africa Company was a state controlled trading organization. See P. Masson, *Histoire des établissements et du commerce français dans l'Afrique barbaresque (1560-1793)* (Paris, 1903).

2. André Siegfried, *Itinéraires de contagion, épidémies et idéologies* (Paris, 1960), pp. 53-60.

3. Ahmad ibn Abi Diyaf, *Athaf ahl az-zaman* (Tunis, 1963-1965), vol.3, pp. 127-29.

4. Archives of the Ministry of Foreign Affairs, Paris.*Correspondance consulaire, Maroc,* vol. 24.

5. Pierre Goubert, *Beauvais et le Beauvaisis de 1600 à 1730, contribution à l'histoire sociale de la France du XVIIe siècle* (Paris, 1960). A similar argument is presented in Goubert's *The Ancien Régime* (New York, 1974), pp. 31-49.

6. Xavier Yacono, "Peut-on évaluer la population de l'Algérie vers 1830?," *Revue Africaine,* no. 98 (1954), pp. 277-307.

7. 'Umar, the second caliph, or successor of Muhammad, ruled the Muslim community during many of the early conquests in the Maghrib (634-644). As his comment suggests, these initial victories in North Africa were hard won.

8. As early as the 9th century, the Abbasid caliphs had begun constituting a corps of mamluks, or white slaves of Turkish and Circassian
extraction purchased with the express objective of becoming part of an
elite military force. Thus, the Moroccan monarch's creation of a slave
bodyguard was by no means unique or unprecedented.

9. Leo Africanus, *The History and Description of Africa* (London,
1600) discusses the location of Moroccan Jews on pages 63, 79, 91, and
204. The later work by Charles de Foucauld is *Reconnaissance du Maroc*
(Paris, 1888).

10. A dynastic rivalry among members of the Tunisian ruling family
resulted in civil war and general instability in the mid-1750s. The Algerians
took advantage of the situation to invade and occupy Tunis, placing a
candidate of their own in power. See Muhammad Saghir ben Yusuf,
Mechra el Melki and Eugène Plantet,*Correspondance des beys de Tunis et
des consuls de France avec la cour, 1577-1830*, 3 vols. (Paris, 1893-99), for
additional details.

2.
An Archaic Society

Myths of Origin

The Awlad* Sidi al-Hani, a tribe settled in the vicinity of the central Tunisian city of Kairouan, claims that its founder came from the Saguia al-Hamra region in the western Maghrib. His six sons started the six segments into which the tribe is now divided. Traditionally, each segment lived in a douar* built around its ancestor's tomb. Another Tunisian tribe, the Awlad Sidi Tlil, claims to have developed in much the same fashion. Sidi Tlil, a descendant of one of the first caliphs, fathered four sons whose progeny compose the four contemporary divisions of the tribe.

There are examples of similar legends in Morocco, including the "epic of the Idma," a tribe of the Seksawa Confederation. Jacques Berque analyzed these Berbers in the 1950s,[1] but the myths about their origin are extremely old and are even expressed in a notarial act, a copy of which dates from the seventeenth century. Tradition says that the tribe was begun by a sharif* from the Moroccan Anti-Atlas region. According to the genealogy, the five sons of Sidi Yahya ibn Muhammad Maghagh came to Usikis over fifteen generations ago and started acquiring territory, sometimes peacefully, but sometimes by force. The present divisions of the Idma living in the villages of Usikis, Ad'erd'ur, and Meghdir are descended from these five immigrants.

Citing additional examples of tribal myths in Algeria or among the sedentary people of the Tunisian Sahel would prove repetitious. An examination of their "histories" reveals the same outline: the migration and settlement of an ancestor, the growth of his family and, occasionally, its spread into other regions. Whether Berber or Arab, sedentary or nomadic, the image which the society has of itself fits a general pattern. The individual is the last link in a genealogical chain and the society is a juxtaposition of many such chains.

These concepts of society emphasize the absence of a perception of the depth of time. History commences only with the founder of the tribe and has no guidelines for dating. It exists outside the lineage context only if the events directly affect the tribe. Beyond the group, reality is nebulous and alien. Therefore, history is closely connected with genealogy and, as a result, begins only with Islam and the Arabs. That there has been history in the Carthaginian, Roman, or Vandal periods is inconceivable. Another characteristic of nonscientific thinking is the confusion of the imaginary and the real. The "miraculous" feats of the tribal holy men become part of the tribe's history, with the natural and the supernatural surviving side by side.

Although the legends of tribal origin have no historical foundation, the tribes stemming more from the consolidation of diverse elements than from the fertility of supposed ancestors, the stories are more than mental constructs, children's tales, or folklore. They determine the cleavages splitting the society. Thus, an exposition of its ethnic composition has been a necessary prerequisite to a discussion of the North African population. When myths of familial ties cannot be preserved, ties based on geographical provenance emerge to replace them. For example, Andalusian families and Livornian Jews retained vivid memories of their emigration from Europe centuries after settling in the Maghrib. Kinship relations within a single tribe — or between groups — although conventional, clearly determine alliances (both political and marital) and conflicts. The origin myth of the Tunisian Mehedhba tribe, for instance, serves to define the boundaries of group solidarity. Of the six children of Sidi Mehedhba, the eponymous ancestor, one established the village of Bou Shemma while another, Hajj Ahmad, was the direct founder of the Mehedhba lineage. This story represents an early effort to forge links between nomads and village dwellers. Hajj Ahmad's descendants eventually moved, breaking down into two segments on Cape Bon. There, quite artificially, were drawn the limits of the tribe's alliance network.

All of these myths are, then, mental projections of very real social structures which concerned every aspect of tribal life, including such critical matters as land distribution, the utilization of the environment, and religious and judicial practices.

Concentric Categories

Let us turn from what is said to what is done. The Berbers of the Moroccan Anti-Atlas analyzed by Robert Montagne[2] constitute one social category. The smallest unit is the hearth, or family. These are the most active segments, contributing to the formation of other larger entities. The hamlet unites from ten to thirty families and four or five hamlets constitute a jamaa't*. Several of these, in turn, make up the major political association, the tribe. An assembly of trusted notables from each village, the anfaliz*, governs the tribe. For all practical purposes, the individual's horizons do not extend beyond the tribe, for within it one marries, settles any legal problems which arise, and fulfills one's religious obligations.

Since the precolonial society was a juxtaposition of many tribes, no single tribe could be completely isolated from the others. There were links of alliance and barriers of enmity between the tribes, particularly since each belonged to a leff* or soff*. Although these alliance systems functioned most visibly in times of crisis, they were not limited to such times. Pilgrimages to the shrines of important saints, for example, often ignored tribal boundaries and united, at least for a limited time, several tribes.

One may ask whether this model applies only to Berber tribes most shielded from outside influences. Certainly the similarity of the Anti-Atlas Berbers' organization to that of Kabylia or the Chaouia is striking.[3] Yet, even among the Algerian, Tunisian, and Moroccan Arabs, although the terminology may have changed, the facts remained the same. In 1790, Lemprière described the Arabs of Morocco as nomads who lived in tents and were, apparently, quite different from the Berbers.[4] Another picture, painted in an 1844 "exposé" of Arab society, exists for Algeria.[5] In both Moroccan and Algerian Arab society the tribe, as defined by links of consanguinity, was at the center of social organization. Endogamy was the norm in both, and unless an individual was related to a group, he could not camp in its douar. The douar housed the agnatic family, including its head, the shaikh*, and his children, relatives, and servants. In political and administrative matters, the assemblage of douar leaders, the jama'a*, acted on issues of concern to the group and safeguarded its interests. The jama'a, by the agreement of its members, designated the most influential chieftain as its leader.

Therefore, the Arabs selected their leaders from the group as a whole, reached decisions by debate among family leaders, and felt a strong sense of tribal solidarity. In short, Arab society was no less "democratic" than that of the mountain Berbers.[6]

Tunisian society presents the same pattern. An 1856 census utilized the same format, with the tribe ('arsh*) at one extreme and the agnatic family at the other. In between were corresponding intermediate units. Even in the villages of the

Sahel, the area most devoid of Berber heritage, the same structure appeared. The population of Moknine, an important city of 5,000 inhabitants in the mid-19th century, undoubtedly reflected the results of endless intermingling. Nevertheless, the city was organized into six groups with outsiders classified according to their ethnic or geographic origin. Tribesmen from the A'radh, Jews, and other groups each had their own shaikh.

The parallels in the societies of all three geographical areas, and in Arab and Berber regions, were nearly absolute. The general theme did, however, receive some chronological and spatial variation, since a village republic may have dominated one area, the douar a second, while in a third the tribe provided the framework for daily life.

Occasionally, allegiance to a soff which had been all but forgotten reemerged. The soff existed everywhere in the Maghrib and neither its strength nor its resiliency should be discounted, as may be shown by a Tunisian example. Between 1729 and 1740, a civil war pitted the bey, Hussain ibn Ali, against his nephew, Ali Pasha. The countryside was split between the two contenders and, using the chronicle of Muhammad Saghir ibn Yusuf, it is possible to determine with which camp the various tribes allied themselves. Nearly a century and a half later, in 1864, a tax revolt swept the country. This uprising against the central government was widespread, but it collapsed quickly as tribes surrendured to the authorities. Of particular note is the fact that the first tribes to yield belonged to the Hussainid, or loyalist, soff, while those which held out longer were from the opposing soff. Tribal divisions continued to follow the same lines of cleavage they had in the 18th century.

From Segmentary Society to Muslim Community

In addition to its function as a political and social unit, the tribe, or one of its components, also served an economic purpose. The procedure used for collecting taxes makes it clear that the tribe had substantial administrative autonomy: the divisions of the tribe shared the tax burden, each segment determining a rate of taxation and seeing to the collection of the money, with this fiscal solidarity assuring the state of its revenues. In judicial matters also, conflict resolution ideally occurred within the tribe or village, either before the council or the judge who was himself a member of the community. When its moral and material interests were at stake, a group might render its own justice, sometimes by the expedient of war against other groups.

When necessary, the option of appealing to the ruler was available, and the bey of Tunis, the dey of Algiers, and the sultan of Morocco all scrupulously filled the role of high judge. Justice at the rulers' tribunals was summary, decisions being made on the spot, and without benefit of preliminary investigations. Sentences were executed with similar dispatch. This justice was also direct, for the litigants appeared before the sovereign without a lawyer.

On the local level, family arbitration did not always work, especially if the parties to a dispute came from different tribes. A dichotomy also arose between customary and Qur'anic law. The problem was most acute in Berber regions of Morocco and Algeria where an individual could set one against the other. Customary law ('urf *) regulated water distribution, provided for the punishment of misdemeanors and, in general, concerned questions affecting the tribe or village as a whole. Qur'anic law involved matters of personal status. In practice, the distinction between the two was not always clear, and the authority of the qadi* sometimes conflicted with the rulings of the jama'a.

In summation, although the society was built around the family model, attachment to a defined political entity (one of the three "states") or to a broad cultural concept (Islam) modified the general schema, making it impossible to view Maghribi society as rigid, closed, or insulated.

The contradiction between insulation and integration into a larger sphere appeared most obviously in religious practices. Normally, an individual's religious life was narrowly circumscribed. Each village had at least one mosque although in the douars this may only have been a tent. The mosque served as a school for the children, symbolized the community's adherence to Islam, and made it possible for the individual to satisfy his religious duties. Throughout the Maghrib, however, the tomb of the local saint was also very much in evidence, complementing as well as contrasting with the mosque. The marabout*, often related to the tribe and sometimes its eponymous founder, translated the social structure described above onto the religious plane. Every tribe acknowledged several marabouts whose tombs were scattered on its territory and who were the objects of more or less fervent devotion by the tribesmen.

The marabouts had important agrarian functions, such as protecting the harvests, and sometimes the tribe stored its grain around the tomb in order to discourage thievery. The shrines were also asylums which not even the sovereign would violate for fear of offending the saint. Frequently, the legends about the saints emphasized their agricultural role, recounting their miracles which had made it possible for the tribe to meet its tax obligations, or explaining how they produced life-giving water in previously unproductive land.

But the marabout had the even more important social function of preserving the cohesion of the group. The cult of the marabouts encouraged large meetings, particularly a yearly pilgrimage just before or after the harvest and votive feasts, the wad'*, during which a shared meal affirmed the solidarity of members of a single tribe or the alliance of unrelated lineages. Finally, the marabout resolved a serious problem by adapting to local requirements the religion of the Muslim ecumene.

There was another facet to religious life in North Africa — the brotherhoods. Unlike the marabouts, the brotherhoods spilled over tribal, village, and alliance boundaries. They brought together adepts from a wide geographical area and represented, as French scholars have maintained, a mechanism through which the individual could break with the normal familial framework of society and choose another. Membership in a brotherhood was an individual, personal decision. It is interesting, for example, that when the founder of the Rahmaniyya Brotherhood, who came from the Djurdjuran Kabylia, died in 1793/1794, the leadership of the order passed not to a member of his family, but to a Moroccan disciple. Extremely active in the late 18th and early 19th centuries, these organizations integrated rural Islam with the remainder of the Muslim community much more effectively than did the marabouts.

They did so only imperfectly, however. In the Maghrib, Islam had failed to obliterate completely certain agrarian rituals which had no Islamic connection. The 'Ashura* ceremony of the Berbers of the High Atlas and Anti-Atlas described by E. Laoust in 1921[7] is one example. Commemorating the death of an old man, the tribesmen participated in a solemn funeral. Then they celebrated his resurrection as a young man whom they married to a fertility ''goddess.'' A love festival during which the clan's marriages took place followed this union. Finally, the fertility ''goddess'' was burned. This ritual of sexuality and fertility, which sought to assure the progression of the seasons, was anathema to orthodox Islam, but far from unique in North Africa. Once again, Berber-speaking regions preserved pre-Islamic religious customs more fully than Arab areas, and rituals such as the one described were less evident in the eastern Maghrib.

In conclusion, this analysis of the social pattern confirms the one proposed by Pierre Bourdieu for Algeria[8] and justifies its extension to all of North Africa. There is no reason to separate Arabs from Berbers, nomads from sedentaries, or maraboutic from nonmaraboutic tribes. All shared the same agnatic, patrilineal family structure. The schema was not so simple, however. Variations occurred, since political and religious concepts independent of the family structure could be superimposed on it. The magnitude of these impositions, coupled with the presence or absence of pre-Islamic vestiges, helps to emphasize contrasts among the three societies. As a general rule, Berber tribes were distinctive in that they retained many characteristics of their pre-Islamic culture including, above all, their language, but also their customary laws and some religious practices which clashed with Islamic orthodoxy. All these factors were obstacles to integration. Of the three regions, Tunisia undoubtedly offered the greatest homogeneity since it was the most totally Arabized, the most deeply Islamized, and the least fragmented geographically. More than Algeria and Morocco, Tunisia had prospects for interchange with other areas and greater prospects for change within itself.

A Classless Society?

One inherent weakness of this schema is its tendency to mask the inequalities which existed in the society's familial organization. There was a difference between tribes which shared in the exercise of power and those which merely submitted to it. All three regions had privileged tribes — the makhzan* in Algeria and Tunisia and the jaish* in Morocco. In return for their military aid to the central government, these tribes received land and enjoyed tax exemptions. Other tribes claimed preeminence in the community by virtue of their ancestry. Whether descended directly from Muhammad (the shurfa*) and the early Arab conquerors, or from maraboutic forebears, such tribes possessed a charisma which distinguished them from the rest of the society.

Moreover, the mechanisms of the family structure itself produced privileged families who dominated the tribe. Power was elective in principle, but if the same family monopolized it for several generations, democracy yielded to less egalitarian forms. In Morocco, Robert Montagne has observed, and sometimes even dated, shifts from participatory democracies to chieftainships.[9] This has been a recent process, coinciding with the reenforcement of the central government in the nineteenth century. In Algeria, on the other hand, the power of such great families as the Muqranis of the Medjana attests to the age of this process.

Finally, the representatives of the government, the governors or qaids*, had all the prerogatives of the ruler but on a smaller scale. Their tenure in office and their relative independence from the sovereign could enable them to become lords not unlike those of the medieval West.

However, nowhere in the Maghrib did there ever emerge the tripartite division of European society so lucidly explained by Georges Dumézil, between the men who prayed, those who fought, and those who worked: *oratores, bellatores, laboratores.* [10] Every Muslim was a potential soldier in the holy war and every healthy man did bear arms — not in the regular army, but within his tribe and for its defense. The makhzan and the jaish tribes may have benefitted from economic privileges, but they had no means of livelihood other than working the land granted to them. Aside from their participation in tax gathering expeditions, they were producers, the same as ordinary tribes.

Even those families claiming nobility through their origins did not always enjoy great wealth. The instability of their power and the quarrels between rival branches of a family heightened the difficulties of social differentiation. A French observer, discussing the various kinds of nobility recognized by the Algerians in 1844, said:

> It would be quite wrong to conclude that all the shorfa, jouad, or marabouts occupy an elevated position in Arab society. On the contrary, they can be seen daily working at every imaginable trade. Nevertheless, if not all members of this class enjoy equally high consideration and influence, it is true that power and authority are restricted to their number.[11]

That being the case, the question arises of whether or not authority over men also constituted control over the land. In other words, in economic terms, were rural holdings subordinated to groups or individuals deemed superior to ordinary tribesmen?

Notes

1. Jacques Berque, *Les Seksawa. Recherches sur les structures sociales du Haut Atlas occidental* (Paris, 1954).

2. Robert Montagne, *Les Berbères et le Makhzen dans le sud du Maroc. Essai sur la transformation politique des Berbères sédentaires (groupe Chleuh)* (Paris, 1930). Many of Montagne's most important findings on Berber society are available in English. See *The Berbers* (London, 1973).

3. The Kabylia is a region of heavy Berber concentration in central and eastern Algeria. The Chaouia is a Berber region in Morocco.

4. William Lemprière, *A Tour from Gibraltar to Tangier, Sallee, Mogadore, and Santa Cruz* (London, 1791), pp. 34-47.

5. Eugène Daumas, *Exposé de l'état actuel de la société arabe* (Algiers, 1844).

6. This is an important point, since much French colonial policy was built around stressing the differences between Berbers and Arabs with the ultimate objective of splitting the two groups against each other and, therefore, facilitating French rule.

7. E. Laoust, "Noms et cérémonies des feux de joie chez les Berbères du Haut et de l'Anti-Atlas," *Hespéris*, I (1921) pp. 3-66, 253-316, and 387-420.

8. Pierre Bourdieu, *Sociologie de l'Algérie*, 3rd Edition (Paris, 1963). An English translation of an earlier edition is entitled *The Algerians* (Boston, 1962).

9. Montagne, *Les Berbères*, pp. 140-45. For a more general survey of Berber political organization, see pp. 119-45.

10. See Georges Dumézil, *L'Idéologie tripartite des Indo-Européens* (Brussels, 1958). For a discussion of Dumézil's work, see C. Scott Littleton, *The New Comparative Mythology* (Berkeley, 1966).

11. Daumas, *Exposé*.

3.
The Rural Economy
as a Household Economy

Awareness of broad tribal groups is important, but an understanding of precolonial North Africa also requires familiarity with the basic organization of the land. To achieve this, the people must be examined in terms of the property they owned or worked and their tools, crops, and herds must also be looked at. Since North Africans were, above all else, peasants — or at least rural people — it is in relation to the land that they can best be comprehended. This undertaking raises such vital questions as who possessed land, who owned the farm implements — and what they were — and who profited from the workers' labors.

From Arboriculture to Nomadism

The bulk of rural activity aimed at satisfying the needs of the immediate society. That was not unusual, since most contemporary rural cultures were, like the Maghrib, subsistence economies. There were, however, many possible forms of rural life, ranging from intensive mixed farming to herding which left only passing marks on the countryside.

The region of Constantine, whose population on the eve of the French conquest André Nouschi has described in detail,[1] provides an example. Several rural patterns coexisted there. The mountaineers of Kabylia and the Aurès were arboriculturists and gardeners producing a variety of fruits and vegetables and olive oil through intensive exploitation of the soil. Enclosed gardens compartmentalized the countryside, and the irrigated soil, enriched with fertilizer, was carefully husbanded by a system of terraces. Despite the scarcity of arable land, Kabyle farmers still managed to grow grains and vegetables. Kabylia was the area, par excellence, of milk* (private, transferable, and inheritable) property.

The Arabs, on the other hand, had immense open lands. They followed one of two occupations: first and foremost was herding (primarily of sheep, although there were more herds of camels in the south), but there was some cultivation of cereals. Each tribe traditionally controlled spacious acreage whose boundaries were recognized by both the sovereign and the neighboring tribes. Membership in the tribe automatically provided access to the land, but the land was not, strictly speaking, collective. Each family worked the plots which it was in a position to cultivate. Although no property titles verified the claims of individual families, their possession of the fields was legitimized by cultivating them, and was continuous and hereditary. So much land for so few people encouraged rotation of crops at irregular intervals. Since the flocks used the land after the harvest and there were no trees or irrigated crops which needed protection from animals, this was, in striking contrast to Kabylia and the Aurès Mountains, a landscape of open fields without water or shade.

The flocks' need for pasturage and the uncertainty of rainfall dictated the rhythm of movements. At the same time, a tribe's location was determined by its dual undertakings of herding and farming. For instance, the Awlad 'Abd al-Nur, from the high plains of Constantine watered by the Wadi*

Rummel, owned fertile lands in the north which they reserved for farming and on which they camped in the summer. After the harvest, however, they migrated to their southern lands which were warmer and more suitable for grazing. The mountain people, then, lived in clusters of huts in permanent communities, while a migratory life style, uniting the tents of an extended family, predominated among the Arabs.

Farther south, on the fringe of the desert, herding was the major livelihood and farming played a negligible part in the economy. The Nementcha, for example, seldom worked in the fields, deriving their wealth from their flocks.

These different types of rural economy may be found, with variations, throughout the Maghrib. Naturally, the produce of the High Atlas arboriculturists, the oasis people, and the villagers of the Tunisian Sahel and Cape Bon are all different, as are the profiles of settlement. Nevertheless, methods of cultivation, types of land tenure, and the molding of the landscape all belong to the same framework.

But do the location and distribution of these life styles correspond to rainfall curves or to the limits of date and olive cultivation? In fact, the correlation is not perfect. Even in Tunisia, nomads were more numerous than villagers as far as the Tell*. But it was not the level of rainfall, the rural activity, or the lack of security which gave rise to that type of settlement in the 19th century. Rather than a result of geographical determinism, it was a legacy of ancient migrations.

The Means of Production

Perhaps even more interesting than the diversity of the rural regions were the shared factors linking them together.

The first common characteristic was the low level of technology. Among both seminomads and arboriculturists, a single agrarian implement was used: the swivel plow. Different models existed throughout the Maghrib, but all were wooden, with only the couplings and the shares made of iron. Such light tools certainly protected the soil and slowed its erosion, but their yield was low and offset these merits. Abbé Poiret, in 1785, described the North African plow as "a simple share attached to a long piece of wood bent in the middle and ending in a yoke."[2] He was depicting the plow of Roman Africa without any modifications.

Could it be said that irrigation techniques, on the other hand, were more refined? Consider this account of the distribution of water at Tozeur:

> Here is the process of the qaddus*: each farmer, when it is his turn to water, takes a cup (qaddus) whose bottom has been pierced with a rather narrow hole which can be plugged with a piece of cord of the kind used to bend the arches in carding. He fills the cup with water and hangs it up somewhere until it is empty. During that time water from one of the canals flows into his garden. The cup is filled a second time and the process is repeated.[3]

Al-Bakri wrote this description in the 11th century, but eight centuries later the system remained unchanged. Sharecroppers working the land still supervised the deviation of water when it was time to irrigate their plots. An observer noted in 1901 that "this method, as primitive as it is, rarely causes disagreements or quarrels"[4] and praised the scheme for allocating water at Tozeur as a masterpiece compared to those employed in neighboring oases.

In keeping with this primitive technology, farmers used sickles to harvest the crops and hand millstones dating from Roman times to grind the grain. Among the herders, the caprices of the climate determined the animals' growth, for they lacked shelter, and reserves of fodder were never planted.

What is most striking overall is the backwardness of technology and tools even in areas thoroughly cultivated by intensive human labor. To compensate for his inability to overcome natural difficulties, the fellah* turned to God or magic, offering prayers for rain, performing rituals when plowing began, or in Kabylia and the High Atlas, setting aside portions of the crop for families believed to have religious powers.

Another trait common to both nomadic and sedentary people was the relatively egalitarian nature of property ownership. Among sedentary groups, the small proprietor and his family owned plots of land jointly with the remainder of the tribe and developed them personally. For example, in 1830 the Ben Shwa haush* near Algiers comprised roughly 840 acres worked by 25 families totaling 85 persons. On the average, each family had about 34 acres of land. Although this was not an appreciable amount, tribesmen also had access to communal lands on which to graze their flocks, as well as to water and wells.

This jointly held family domain was hardly an isolated case. It typified not only the entire Algerian Sahel and the Mitidja[5] (where the average family holding was less than 25 acres), but also Kabylia and Tunisian villages in the Sahel and the vicinity of Bizerte and Cape Bon. Throughout these areas, families owned small plots of cultivable land whose meagre resources were complemented by the family's right to such collective property as forests, meadows, and pastures.

The available figures suggest that land distribution was no different within the tribes. 1873 statistics covering 402 tribes reveal that 77 percent of the families possessed less than 25 acres of arable land, while 21 percent had between 25 and 100 acres. The pastures were collective. A similar pattern prevailed among the tribes of the Tunisian steppe.

There were, however, some large estates which the owners could not develop without help. This category included the hubus* lands, or property turned over to mosques or marabouts; the property of the ruler and important families; and farms owned by city residents. The existence of these estates implies the existence of some landless peasants.

The extent of these domains is a major consideration in

assessing the number of such peasants, but it has never been measured. The prevalence of hubus land varied considerably from region to region, and in Algeria it was uncommon around Tenès, Cherchell, and Constantine. In any case, hubus land belonging to a zawiya* was normally worked by the maraboutic family. If not, it was at least left for the use of other families, conditional only on the payment of a minimal tax. Hubus foundations, therefore, did not always necessitate the labor of landless peasants. Indeed, the hubus was often a form of defense against possible usurpation by the government or powerful neighbors, since the donor's family retained use of the land, and as long as the family line continued, it would be sacrilegious to deprive them of it.

The rulers managed their estates in a variety of ways. Sometimes neighboring tribes cultivated them under a corvée system, occasionally the sovereign rented them to tenant farmers, and in still other instances, khammas* (sharecroppers) worked the land. The owner provided the khammas with land, a team, and seeds, and for their labor the khammas received a fifth of the harvest.

Major landlords resorted to the same procedures. Although not very numerous, tenant farmers and sharecroppers can be classed as landless peasants, some of whose labor benefitted nonworking property owners rather than themselves. In the Constantinois, such poor peasants probably made up less than 20 percent of the population. Moreover, some rural people worked rented land as well as the acreage they had inherited. In pre-protectorate Tunisia, only immigrants or peasants separated from their families worked as khammas.

Before the population growth of the 20th century, there was no rural proletariat to speak of in the Maghrib, where small land owners and small family farms predominated.

Thus, a home-oriented economy, to which the social unit turned for the satisfaction of its vital needs, flourished. The land provided food; the women wove clothing, such furnishings as rugs and covers, and if the family lived in a tent, even its home. They fashioned kitchen utensils, dishes, couscoussiers*, and a host of objects of glazed earthenware. In general, people were satisfied with very little. Clothes were plain and food was simple, with coffee and tea considered luxuries.

At the same time, the economy was far from autarkic. Quite the contrary: trade was a prerequisite for survival. At the local level, technological inadequacy contrasted sharply with the sophisticated organization of internal group solidarity, the latter compensating for the former and also counteracting the small tracts being farmed by most rural people. For example, if a peasant was hard pressed after a bad harvest or an outbreak of epizootic disease in his flock, he went to the qaid on market day and explained his situation. The qaid then summoned the shaikhs and other influential men in order to fix a time for a ma'una* (a meeting for mutual assistance) at the peasant's home. On the appointed day, the peasant served a meal for his guests. After an evening of singing and dancing, one man stood in the center of the throng and accepted donations, loudly announcing the name of the contributor and the amount of his gift. At daybreak the alms were counted and the guests departed.

Similar reciprocities were common, including assistance in the fields when a family lacked sufficient manpower, meetings of women to grind the grain, and the loan of tools and implements.

These occasional demonstrations of solidarity helped guarantee family survival, but even more important were the strict and complex regulations protecting each group's rights. Thus, the administration of the fortified collective granaries bordering the desert from Morocco to Tripolitania and the distribution of water in the oases were both stringently regulated by customs, some of which were systematically codified (see Document 10, page 000), while others remained oral. The harsher the climate and the more irregular the resources, the more minute was the management of daily life.

An Open Economy

On a broader plane, there was a division of labor between local economies, each complementing the others. Sugar, for instance, entered the Maghrib through foreign trade only in small quantities. The oasis dwellers, purveyors of dates, provided it, and the gathering, transporting, and sale of dates stimulated regular, vital currents of exchange. For example, the Arb·, Saharan nomads, came north in summer to pasture their flocks, bringing with them dates and products from their herds (sheep, goat and camel hair, and wool) which they bartered for grain. Each Arb· clan traded with certain tribes in the Tell, temporarily settling among them. Then, in autumn, the nomads returned south. This regular trade laid the foundation for the close linkages between nomads and settled people which characterized the North African economy. A similar complementarity of interests associated villagers with the seminomads of the plateaux. The former, whether mountaineers or Sahelians, supplied fruits, oil, or handicrafts; the latter, grain. Annual meetings, and more frequent markets, permitted exchanges which supplied the deficit of local economies while simultaneously giving the groups an opportunity to renew their alliance bonds.

Conflicts could develop, but these contacts generally served as regulators of rural life. Rural relationships with the cities were quite different. Country people acquired luxury commodities such as colonial produce and the products of local industry (fine cloth, saddles, leather goods, weapons, and jewelry) in urban markets. The peasant came to the city to offer his services, seeking temporary work. He provided the city with the fruits of his labor, feeding its population by provisioning its markets and augmenting foreign trade, since the Maghrib exported rural products to Europe. Finally, through his taxes, the peasant supported the state and its army.

Indeed the fiscal system weighed most heavily on the rural population. Based on the Qur'an, it was similar in all three countries. The primary tax was the tithe on all agrarian wealth including grain, oil, and flocks. Joined to the 'ushr* (tenth) were other taxes which varied from tribe to tribe and region to region. Examples were occupancy taxes, personal levies, and requirements for corvées. One of these impositions, the tithe, was collected in kind, and revenues from all of them went, in part, to the soldiers who collected them and the qaids and notaries who assessed them. Since the central government did not pay regular salaries to its agents, they took their pay from what was extracted from the taxpayers. Consequently, funds thinned noticeably before reaching the state's coffers, and the amount collected cannot be evaluated.

Nevertheless, all other taxes paled in comparison with those inflicted on rural citizens. The total amount of the capitation tax on Jews who, as has been seen, were not very numerous, the customs and commercial taxes, special income derived from exactions on vacant estates, and the tribute paid by Christian nations to maintain peace, did not equal the revenue from a tax which fell on all producers and their products. This was obvious even to contemporary foreigners like Shaler¹ who, in trying to calculate the dey's funds, estimated those originating in the countryside at more than half the total.

Even when popular resistance and the administration's own mediocrity lowered the revenue collected, the peasantry still bore the brunt of the fiscal burden. Through the tax system, the state, its agents, and its army took of the peasants' labor virtually everything they did not consume directly.

Should precolonial North Africa be characterized as a feudal, archaic, or class society? The existence of great estates and of powerful families able to obtain, by virtue of their influence, corvées from subjects suggests that Maghribi society was indeed feudal. Yet the process of feudalization appears not to have gone so far as to alter the body of social relationships. Until the colonial period, for instance, North

African peasants kept both their land and their arms. Disparities in wealth and prestige in no way changed this basic fact.

The distribution of property, as well as its extent and the methods by which it was exploited, demonstrate, in the final analysis, the equilibrium of precolonial North African society. They also reflect its length and its stagnation, since the society's ability to satisfy its elementary needs prevented the rise of tensions or inequalities which would have demanded change.

Notes

1. André Nouschi, *Enquête sur le niveau de vie des populations rurales constantinoises de la conquête jusqu'en 1919* (Paris, 1961).

2. Abbé Poiret, *Voyage en Barbarie* (Paris, 1789), p.74

3. al-Bakri, *Kitab al-Masalik*. A French translation of this geographical treatise is *Description de l'Afrique septentrionale* (Algiers, 1857-58).

4. J. Brunhes, *L'Irrigation, ses conditions géographiques, ses modes et son organisation dans la péninsule ibérique et dans l'Afrique du Nord* (Paris, 1902).

5. The Mitidja was the rich fertile plain behind Algiers where much of the agrarian life of the country was concentrated both before and during the colonial period.

6. William Shaler, *Sketches of Algiers, Political, Historical, and Civil* (Boston, 1826). Shaler, one of the most perceptive English-speaking observers of the precolonial Maghrib, was the United States' representative in Algiers from 1815 until 1827.

4.
The City: Turning Inward
or Seeking External Contacts?

The city, a Tower of Babel, was certainly the most complex
organism in Maghribi society. In addition to being more
varied ethnically and linguistically than other regions, the
cities were also the scenes of the Maghrib's most obvious
social contrasts. What did the lower classes of the suburbs of
Tunis have in common with the city's notables? Did a let-
tered citizen of Fez and a poor craftsman of the same city
share any important experiences? Turks and corsair captains, distinguished by their splendid apparel, contrasted
sharply with the Biskri porters of Algiers. A man's quality
was judged by the shape, the folds, the color, and the material of his turban. Adding to this complexity, the city
provided a variety of services, with every trade and every
commodity, the man of the law and the man of science,
represented there.

This flourishing urban life affected only a fraction of the
population, however. Fez, Marrakesh, and Meknes all
served as capitals of Morocco, but even the most important,
Fez, had less than 100,000 residents. In the whole country,
the urban population constituted much less than 20 percent
of the total. Even so, the ports of Tangiers, Tetouan, and

Mogador, as well as Taroudant, the capital of the Sous region, were cities of several thousand people. In Algeria, the insignificance of urban life was more apparent. Over 90 percent of the population lived in rural areas. Except for Constantine (population about 25,000), the eastern part of the country had no important cities. Central Algeria was more highly urbanized, but at the time of the French conquest Algiers contained at most 50,000 people, while Blida, Médéa, and Miliana were very small towns. In the west, Tlemcen had only 20,000 citizens and Mascara even fewer. Cities were more common in Tunisia. The most reasonable estimates place the population of the capital at 120,000, or double that of Algiers. Small but bustling cities such as Bizerte, Sousse, Monastir, Mahdia, and Sfax dotted the coast, while cities or market centers could be found in the hinterland as well. These included Béja and Gafsa as well as Kairouan, the old religious metropolis whose handicraft business had declined considerably. Despite this urban network in Tunisia, the population of all the cities represented less than a fifth of the total. Although figures are necessarily approximate, they are quite revealing. The rural population of the Maghrib greatly exceeded the urban population and the agrarian sector of the economy took precedence over the urban sector.

The Structure of the City

The distinction in North Africa between cities and towns or villages seems less clear than in the West. Villages were often fortified, and the presence of mosques, public baths, and sometimes even a specialized craft industry, likened such communities to the cities. Conversely, orchards surrounded the cities and sometimes grew within its confines, as at Rabat and Fez Djedid.[1] Some city people owned or worked garden plots, giving Sousse, Tunis, Algiers, and Fez the appearance of oases. Life style — urbanity or rusticity — established the boundary between city and town more than did the function of each entity.

Moreover, the concept of the family, on which the entire social system was built, also existed in the city, and although its norms were applied with more discretion than in the country, it still retained its effectiveness. Throughout the Maghrib, the physical features of the cities were similar. At the base was the home, a small component of urban life. It was a family structure with many separate rooms united around a courtyard. Shielded from prying eyes by a blind façade and a zig-zag entryway, it housed a single family. Multifamily dwellings were unknown, as were buildings combining living quarters with a workshop or store. There was complete functional segregation.

Ethnic divisions existed side by side with this functional segregation. Each quarter consisted of a maze of houses whose occupants were linked by bonds of kinship rather than neighborly sociability. In Algiers, the Moors, longstanding city dwellers, did not mix with the Kabyles, and Berber Hadris in Tlemcen deemed it unthinkable to live among the Couloughlis. Fez had Kairawin and Andalusian quarters, while newcomers settled in the barrani*, the foreign "community." Even the smaller cities, such as Bizerte, were similarly segmented. In accordance with these traditions, Jews clustered in their own quarters. Nevertheless, ethnic segregation was not absolute, for the cities had experienced too many transformations to permit categorical observation of ethnic exclusiveness.

The neighborhood, in this urban organization, served an overwhelmingly residential function. Common facilities were reduced to a minimum: a mosque, a communal oven, but never a business or a workshop. If they were found, they were relegated to a single street, making it a replica of the principal suq*. Narrow streets traversed this residential area, forming corridors leading to a single exit. In these circumstances, the street was actually part of the dwelling, resulting in a maze of dead ends and blind alleys which European observers, used to seeing streets as means of circulation and exchange, considered bad mistakes. The privacy of the streets is illustrated even more strikingly by the Algerian practice, which Shaler reported, of closing the gates of each quarter at nightfall.

The locus of the urban community was its center, where both the market and the main mosque were situated. At Fez Djedid the palace occupied the central space, but this exception can be explained by the origin of Fez Djedid and its military purpose. At Fez Bali the general rule prevailed, with the zawiya of Moulay Idris, the city's founder; the Kairawin mosque; and the suqs at the center, making it both the religious and economic core of Fez. Generally speaking, other North African cities had similar patterns.

In addition to an acute division of labor in the urban markets, professions were often organized along ethnic and geographic lines. Each trade had its own street and one ethnic group specialized in it. In Fez, Algiers, and Constantine, only Jews worked with precious metals, while the porters of Fez were always Berbers from the Middle Moulouya region. Recruited from the same families and tribes, they wore distinctive costumes and worked under the supervision of their own amin*. Leo Africanus noted this situation, which was rediscovered by Roger LeTourneau in the 20th century.[2] In Algiers, only Mzabites operated mills and bakeries, while Biskris were either porters or managers of public baths. The Djerid and Djebel Matmata supplied Tunis with laborers, water carriers, and masons. The capital's chechia industry was regarded as Andalusian in origin, continued by descendants of Spanish exiles. In reality, however, this was not true. Of the more than 150 owners of chechia businesses in 1809-1810, only a minority were of Andalusian stock, and many came from the Ottoman Empire or Tunisia itself. The most powerful families — the Lakhwas, the Louzirs, and the Sidhas — were, however, Andalusian. As in other instances, ethnic unity and family ties were more imaginary than real, but they were vigorously claimed nonetheless.[3]

Laid out in this fashion, there were no main squares or open public spaces and, therefore, nothing which served as a symbol for the community of city dwellers. The expression of public opinion took place only in the mosque, an enclosed area which duplicated the family dwelling, serving as a reminder that the first mosque resulted from improvements made on the Prophet's house.

Robert Brunschvig, studying "Medieval Urbanism and Muslim Law," wrote: "It was family considerations which, in all matters, took precedence."[4] The precolonial Maghrib's primary orientation was domestic.

Urban Professions and Indigenous Capitalism

Urban society was preindustrial as well as prepolitical. The vitality of the trades is somewhat deceptive, for the production of luxury goods absorbed a disproportionate amount of labor. Craftsmen met only the needs of the city or, at most, of the region. Thus, pottery from Tetouan and hats from Fez or Algiers were sold throughout Morocco. A few products, such as the babouches* made by leather workers in Tetouan and Fez, and the fine leather goods from Rabat and Tetouan, were more widely distributed. Woolen cloth from the Djerid and Djerba and silk belts from Algiers were exported to all of North Africa and even the Middle East. Europe sought such selected items as *scialamecchini,* or fine wool, which Tunisian ships carried to Livorno. Merchants there sent it on to Poland, where local Jews used it to make prayer shawls.

Even in businesses involved in "international" commerce, there were no alterations in the methods of workmanship. Hand labor, performed in small workshops staffed by a master (mu'allim*) assisted by a few workers and apprentices, still prevailed. Each trade had a supervisor (amin) who oversaw the quality of the craftsmanship and settled conflicts between owners and their employees or the heads of competing firms. On the city-wide level, the muhtasib* policed the markets to control prices. This structure existed throughout the Maghrib and was identical to that used in Muslim cities in the Middle Ages. Productivity depended on human energy rather than machines and the worker's skill counted more than his output.

One business, although organized along traditional lines, was a major industry — the manufacturing of chechias in Tunis. Even a traveller like MacGill, attuned to the trans= formations under way in the English textile industry, observed the magnitude of this trade. The variety and quality of the Tunisian chechias partially, though not entirely, accounted for the craft's importance.

An acute division of labor characterized the production of this article. Making a single chechia required dozens of operations, each performed by a highly specialized artisan. First the wool was sorted, cleaned, and spun; then women in a village near Tunis knitted it into cloth. The fulling process took place in Tebourba, after which the material was returned to the workshop for carding and clipping. Before finishing and conditioning, the material had to be dyed at Zaghouan and carded in the workshop a second time. A master in Tunis oversaw the shipping and processing of the raw material, assigning the jobs and coordinating the independent craftsmen. This kind of operation typifies early industrial capitalism. Similar enterprises existed in France at the same time.

Thus, a comparison between Europe and North Africa is in order. A French industry manufacturing "Tunis-style" caps attempted to supplant the regency in the Levantine market. Production mechanisms at Marseille were clearly artisanal. Prior to the Revolution, and still at the end of the Empire, less than ten firms, employing very few laborers, divided the work. But in Aix from 1787, and in Orléans from even earlier, much larger concerns, some of them employing forty of fifty workers in a single building, dominated production. The work methods of even these large businesses were no different. Their equipment was rudimentary, generally consisting of tools rather than machines. Although these firms minimized the transportation of raw material and executed many more operations in the factory, they still relied on scattered workers. Moreover, the process of work had not yet deteriorated to the point at which artisans became simply factory workers, losing their special skills.

The Tunisian government made a pretense of preventing the development of monopolies by guaranteeing an equitable division of such raw material as wool from Segovia and vermilion, but, nevertheless, disparities could be discerned among the businesses. The 1809-1810 distributions, whose records have been preserved by chance, indicate that some workshops could process substantial quantities of wool. Since quality chechia production required many workers, large businesses must have existed, thereby providing a comparison with French industry.

In spite of French and Italian competition, Tunisia exported chechias throughout the Ottoman Empire from Tripolitania to Bulgaria, as well as to the western Maghrib and sub-Saharan Africa, producing 50,000 to 100,000 dozen annually. This Tunisian industry clearly stands up well when compared with similar European industries of the time.

The sale of the regency's goods stimulated widespread commerce conducted either by temporary companies or by individuals supervising the entire exchange circuit. For example, in 1814 a Tunis merchant bought oil and shipped it to Spain where he purchased fine wool with its sale price. He distributed the wool in Tunis in exchange for chechias which he exported to his agent in Alexandria. From Egypt he received merchandise and a letter of credit. This procedure took almost three years to complete, but the profits realized at each stage more than satisfied the merchant's expectations. Knowing the needs of the regions with which he did business, offering credit to masters for whom he provided raw material, receiving promises of payment, and keeping accounts, this man was certainly a capitalist merchant, every bit as competent in his affairs as his Marseillais or Italian counterparts.

The growth of commercial and industrial capitalism in Tunisia, a Muslim country, corresponded to the degree of Europe's industrialization. Was Tunisia an exception in this regard among Muslim countries supposedly hostile to modern economic structures? In reality, the notion of Islam opposing capitalism is a myth, though one which has defenders even today. In the present, as in the past, Islam resists capitalism in neither theory nor practice. (A selection in Appendix 2 of this book summarizes the controversy over Islam's role in economic development.) This overview of a major Tunisian industry and the commerce to which it gave rise verifies the presence of a capitalist sector in a Muslim country well before the advanced European economy burst onto the North African scene. Moreover, it is unlikely that the chechia industry was an isolated case. No other business in the Maghrib served so vast a market, but the most extensive industries of Algeria and Morocco — leather and textiles — undoubtedly had many parallels with it. Although they have left less evidence of their activity, they belonged to a capitalist sector of the economy, produced for the market place, and had entrepreneurs overseeing the work of several artisans. Nevertheless, capitalism affected only a secondary sector of the economy, which was largely untouched by it. Moreover, no new undertakings early in the 19th century succeeded these traditional professions. The industrial revolution entailed use of the steam engine plus the machine tool, and these were unknown in North Africa. The most advanced industries underwent internal changes such as mechanization or the development of more rational production methods. Subsequent changes, such as the shrinkage of the market, livelier competition, and changes in clothing styles, were all external; they provoked no attempts at adaptation nor did they shake the social structures of North African industry from their inertia.

The Caravan Trade

The foregoing assessment of manufacturing's stagnation is also applicable to the caravan trade. On the surface, it retained its vitality since commerce with Black Africa, the traffic within the Maghrib, and exchanges with Egypt and the holy cities of Mecca and Medina all depended on overland arteries.

Several routes led to Black Africa. From Morocco, the most important was the salt road following the Wadi Noun to the southern reaches of the kingdom and continuing to Ouadane where the caravan secured salt. It then proceeded to Timbuktu and Djenné, where the Moroccans traded their salt for gold, ostrich feathers, ivory, and slaves. A more westerly approach went through Tafilalt, and each year one caravan travelled this ancient highway of the spice and gold trade. Both trips took roughly fifty days.

In Tunisia and Algeria, tribes specializing in desert transport dominated the trans-Saharan trade. To the west, the Shaamba carried merchandise south to El-Goléa or Timimoun, and in Tunisia, the Ourghemma loaded merchandise in Gabès for shipment to Ghadamès. South of these outposts, the Tuaregs[5] linked North African tribes with commercial centers as far away as Timbuktu.

On the whole, however, all of this traffic was unimpressive. For one thing, mercantile techniques were unsophisticated. Even though credit was unknown, currency rarely appeared as a method of payment. The Moroccans paid in surra* (purses of gold dust) when they dealt with Timbuktu. As a rule, barter prevailed over commerce, and in the 1790s a belt or a salt tablet sufficed to purchase a Bambara slave. Exchanges depended on the extreme economic and technological retardation of Black Africa.

In addition, the volume of commerce was modest and the caravans infrequent. Expeditions following the Moroccan salt route left only every second or third year and the meager goods in the shops of Tlemcen, a principal entrepôt for products from the African interior, astonished foreign observers. Algiers had no direct contacts with the sub-Saharan regions, but once a year a Jew journeyed to the edge of the desert with three mules laden with grain. He returned with ostrich feathers and a small quantity of gold dust. The Constantine caravan was merely a branch of the Tunis-Ghadamès caravan, which itself made only a trip or two a year and was not regarded in Tunis as overly important. This trade also supplied very little, transporting ostrich plumes, senna, gum from the Sudan, and slaves north. For these goods, Tunisia traded European textiles and colonial merchandise as well as its own products including chechias, burnouses, and fine woolen cloth. Algeria and Morocco exported foodstuffs and also received similar goods from Black Africa. For all three countries, only the traffic in slaves made the caravans worthwhile: each year Morocco imported several thousand slaves, and Algeria and Tunisia several hundred.

The trans-Saharan trade was, then, a regular but unspectacular one. It followed classic routes and was static from at least the beginning of the 18th century and probably earlier.

East-west traffic served a quite different purpose. The most important caravan was the pilgrimage caravan carrying Muslims to Mecca. North Africans joined it by the thousands, accompanied by untold numbers of camels. Assembling in Taza, in Morocco, the pilgrim caravan crossed Algeria and Tunisia, via either the Djerid or Tunis. Bulging with travellers from the regencies, it reached Tripolitania after a trip of more than two months. After regrouping there, the caravan resumed its journey to Alexandria, arriving forty or fifty days later. When the pilgrim finally reached Mecca, no matter how devout he was, he participated in the huge trade fair which united Muslims from every corner of the world. Muslins and silks from the Levant, rich Persian cloth, amber, and spices changed hands in return for wool, babouches, chechias, and even Black slaves brought to

Mecca by the North Africans. On the return trip, the pilgrim could acquire raw silk or cotton in Cairo. At the completion of the pilgrimage the hajj* had journeyed over 4,000 miles round trip from Tunisia to Mecca and over 6,000 if he had started in Taza. By Lemprière's estimate, he had also more than doubled his initial capital.[6] These vagabonds were merchant-pilgrims accompanying their goods to a great fair. Their undertaking required both audacity and fortitude, but the assurance of saving their souls more than compensated for the risk of being murdered en route or dying of the plague or exhaustion. In Europe, conversely, this type of itinerant commerce had ceased centuries earlier.

Trade between the various regions of North Africa was more common than the annual pilgrimage caravan to Mecca, but North African merchants used identical trade techniques. As with other overland commerce, inter-Maghribi trade depended on the high prices of luxury products to offset its small volume. A monthly caravan of two or three hundred mules loaded with embroidered clothes, belts, and fabrics travelled between Constantine and Tunis, returning with rugs from Asia Minor, silk from Syria, and coffee.

The caravan trade with Black Africa and other portions of the Muslim world unquestionably helped maintain the animation of urban crafts; created additional sources of income in places, such as the Djerid or Gabès, used as stopovers or storage facilities; and enriched the merchants of Fez, Tlemcen, and Tunis. It is equally certain that its decline and eventual disappearance in the 19th century further aggravated the social disequilibrium of the Maghrib. Early in the 19th century, however, commerce was too inadequate to create a strong industrial or mercantile bourgeoisie or to enliven a firmly set economy. Following the oldest routes and using the oldest methods known in the Muslim world, the caravan trade could not rejuvenate the entire economy.

As often happened, differences within the Maghrib existed, as between Morocco in "splendid isolation" and Tunisia with strong commercial interests. The former undertook no regular relations with other Muslim countries aside from the caravans previously noted and a few boats transporting pilgrims to Mecca. The latter, on the other hand, nurtured an interest in maritime commerce as well as in overland trade. For the moment, this aspect of trade can be ignored, for it should be analyzed in terms of its confrontation with European foreign trade, a subject which will be considered later.

Notes

1. The city of Fez was actually two cities, Fez Bali and Fez Djedid, built side by side. Fez Djedid (New Fez) was a later addition, erected primarily for military and administrative purposes. See Roger LeTourneau, *Fez in the Age of the Marinids* (Norman, Oklahoma, 1961), pp. 15-34.

2. Leo Africanus, *Description,* p. 432. Pages 393-606 in this fascinating period piece are a general description of the city of Fez. The LeTourneau work referred to is *Fès avant le protectorat* (Casablanca, 1949), although mention is also made of these circumstances in *Fez in the Age of the Marinids,* pp. 30, 51-52.

3. On the chechia industry's extremely important place in Tunisian economic growth see Lucette Valensi, "Islam et capitalisme: production et commerce des chechias en Tunisie et en France au XVIIIe siècle et XIXe siècle," *Revue d'Histoire Moderne et Contemporaine,* 16 (July-September 1969), pp. 376-400.

4. Robert Brunschvig, "Urbanisme médiéval et droit musulman," *Revue d'Etudes Islamiques,* 1947, pp. 127-55.

5. The Shaamba, Ourghemma, and Tuaregs were all tribesmen of the Saharan region whose principal means of survival was the caravan trade, either through plundering it or guiding it through the desert wastes.

6. Lemprière, *A Tour,* p. 352.

5.
The North Africans and the Sea

What of maritime commerce? Since both Christian contemporaries and later historians have frequently depicted the regencies of Algiers and Tunis as states thriving on piracy, it is imperative to begin any study of maritime commerce by examining the myth of the Barbary threat and gauging the dimensions of the corsair phenomenon.

The Absence of Merchant Fleets

First, a most important fact: those sea-rovers had no merchant marine. The Europeans prevented such developments by blocking efforts to create commercial fleets or establish direct Muslim trade with Christian countries.

Corsairs armed by the Knights of Malta[1] or flying the flag of the Two Sicilies harassed North African commerce and maintained a state of constant insecurity until the late 18th century. Jacques Godechot's research reveals the following figures of prizes taken to Malta from the Barbary states between Tripolitania and eastern Algeria:

1764	204 seizures
1770	2 seizures
1775	94 seizures
1780	240 seizures
1785	157 seizures
1788	78 seizures[2]

Moreover, between 1780 and 1789, the Christians took to Malta some 500 Muslims captured off the Tunisian coast, to which number 468 more Muslims were added between 1790 and 1798. The Gulf of Zuara, the waters off Djerba and the Kerkennah Islands, the Gulf of Hammamet, the Gulf of Tunis, and Cape Serrat were hunting grounds for Christian privateers. Their presence not only prevented international commerce, but also hampered coastal trade and fishing along the entire Tunisian shoreline.

Such Christian privateering was of only minor economic importance in terms of the prizes taken. Even at Malta, the island's role as a Mediterranean commercial entrepôt outweighed its significance as the headquarters of the Order of Saint John. Privateering did, however, help protect Christian commerce from Muslim competition and Marseille businessmen encouraged it for that reason, if no other. France's chargé d'affaires in Malta made this quite clear when he said in 1790:

> The continued prosperity of Marseille's trade, which provides the Order with substantial tokens of concern for it, requires that we attempt to keep the Turks from carrying their merchandise on their own vessels, thus keeping them dependent on us.[3]

As a further proof of the Christian corsairs' negative impact on North African trade, Tunisian ships began to appear at Malta after the Knights were abolished in 1798. Nineteen vessels sailed there in 1800 and six more arrived in the first seven months of 1801. A few Tunisian captains even ventured to Livorno after 1809 and by 1814 about twenty had made the voyage. These figures are small, but they underscore the inhibiting role of European privateers.

Marcel Emerit has demonstrated the restrictive effect of the Inquisition on Maghribi commerce.[4] Since many of the rais* — ship captains — were Christian renegades who had converted to Islam in the hope of growing rich or winning rapid social prominence, they risked prison or torture if they returned to Christian countries. Examples of such mishaps occurred as late as the 18th century.

Under these circumstances, it is hardly surprising that the North Africans continued to turn to privateering to acquire resources denied them through legitimate commerce. Eventually Europeans recognized this dilemma and a few isolated voices proposed means of alleviating it. Some contemporaries suggested giving merchant vessels to the Maghribi governments. A report issued in Venice recommended opening Europe's ports to North Africans, arguing that commerce would lead to the renunciation of privateering. The report added that it would be necessary to go to war if the Muslims were obdurate, but the author optimistically contended that ''whoever seeks humanity in man finds him the same in all nations and in every climate.''[5]

The permanence of Christian privateering and the West's resistance to commercial penetration from the Maghrib, therefore, encouraged corsair activity. Another effect of these attitudes — the relegation of North Africa's seaborne trade to Christian carriers — will be discussed below. Privateering, at least in Algiers and Tunis, enjoyed its last phase of prosperity at the end of the 18th century.

The Closing Era of Barbary Privateering

Morocco no longer posed any danger. By the close of the 17th century the Salé corsairs had been subjugated and privateering had ended. Even as a state business, privateering had declined steadily. Moulay Muhammad ibn 'Abdullah tried to revive it, but even when the Moroccan fleet appeared to have resumed some vitality in 1764, it consisted of only two frigates, a corvette, two shabbaks*, and ten sloops of war. Under Moulay Slimane (1792-1822), the corsair fleet disappeared entirely and by 1818 Rabat housed only one dilapidated ship which the sultan presented to Algiers in 1820. Moulay Slimane's successor again showed some inclination to rebuild the fleet, but Austrian reprisals for the seizure of some vessels destroyed the Moroccan ships at Larache in 1829.

Unlike its neighbors, Morocco reaped no profits from the insecurity reigning in the Mediterranean during the Napoleonic wars. In Algiers and Tunis, the Mediterranean's entanglement in large scale warfare allowed the rais to concentrate on the holy war with renewed fervor. Although privateering had centered around Algiers at the beginning of the 17th century, by the end of the 18th, the dey's capital had lost its superiority over Tunis and Tripoli, the former city assuming dominance. In Algiers privateering was the business of the state. The bey was the principal shipowner. The wakil al-kharidj* (minister of the navy)[6] launched only one vessel and there were no other owners. In Tunis, on the other hand, neither the state nor the Turks monopolized privateering. Major government figures such as the kahiya* of Porto Farina and the keeper of the seal, as well as such businessmen as the Djelloulis from Sfax or the Ben Ayads and Hajj Yunis ibn Yunis from Djerba, all participated in outfitting a fleet of privateers. The result was twofold. First, the Tunisian fleet regained the strength it had had at the peak of privateering in the first quarter of the 17th century. Tunis then owned fifteen to thirty mighty warships and there was an equal number late in the 18th century. Secondly, Tunisian power surpassed that of its neighbors. The precise number of ships outfitted by Tunis is difficult to assess because the rais did not always command the same vessel and the various kinds of ships are poorly differentiated in archival records. The same boat is listed as a bark in one reference but as a polacre in another. The number of raids, which approached one hundred in 1798, is more easily ascertainable. At the same time, Algiers had only ten or twenty warships, a far cry from the seventy-five sails the city had mustered in 1623.

The Algerian fleet was not growing at the end of the 18th century. Indeed, the list of seizures published by Devoulx[7] indicates the relative stability of the fleet's strength since the third quarter of the 18th century. Privateering in Algiers owed its renewed vigor more to circumstances in Europe than to any other factor. The number of raids executed by each ship and the daring of their captains compensated for the small number of vessels. For example, Rais Hamidu captured a Portuguese forty-four gun frigate with 282 men aboard in 1802.

The Tunisians performed similar spectacular exploits. In 1798 they captured the entire population of an island near Sardinia, enslaving about a thousand people. In 1815 they seized another 125 Christians at St. Antiochus.[8]

In the long run, the profits of privateering balanced out between the two regencies. More than 1,500 slaves entered Algiers from 1802 to 1815, while the number of Christian captives in Tunis was similar. In both countries the slaves were most often subjects of Naples or Sardinia.

The two countries were similar in other areas as well — procedures for outfitting ships, the division of spoils, and the treatment of slaves. Europe furnished such raw material as iron, wood, and ammunition. Although there were a few North African sailors, most of the seaman came from the Ottoman Empire, particularly Albania, Candia, and other rugged coastal regions where destitution forced men to the sea. Shipowners in Algiers and Tunis bore the same expenses. In addition to the boat and its equipment, they provided stores of wheat, rice, olives, oil, vinegar, coffee, and, occasionally, meat.

In Tunis, an association reminiscent of the Italian merchants' commenda[9] sometimes shared outfitting costs. Established for one voyage only, the society dissolved itself after a pro rata division of the booty according to each investor's capital outlay. Private outfitting and associations of investors required methods of sharing profits different from those utilized in Algeria. For example, when the bey did not participate in equipping a vessel, he received only a tenth of the booty but had a preemptive right to captives whom he could acquire cheaply. The shipowner retained any vessels seized, which meant he could maintain his strength at the expense of the infidel. The Portuguese frigate which Hamidu captured was quickly launched against the Christians, for instance. The booty, including captives, was evaluated and the owner received half. The remaining half was the crew's share, which was divided according to each man's rank and his job during the voyage.

In Tunis only those who contributed to the cruise's success with either capital or manpower shared in the profits, but in Algiers many individuals benefitted from privateering, if only in a small way. The minister of the navy and his assistant, the agent responsible for surveillance of the port, the qaid al-marsa* who met ships arriving in Algiers, the pilots who guided the ships through the entrance to the port, and two shawushes*, one Muslim and the other Jewish, were all entitled to share in the prizes. Even the marabouts could lay claim to a portion of the booty. The sale of captured merchandise employed guards, porters (always from Biskra), criers, measurers, weighers, and loaders. Paying all these costs absorbed as much as 15 percent of the voyage's profits.

In Algiers, then, the entire society benefitted from privateering although not everyone depended on it exclusively. The ransoming of slaves provided their masters and their intermediaries, normally Jews, with a final opportunity for financial gain. The bey of Tunis, for example, realized a handsome profit of 100 to 200 percent on the liberation of Christian prisoners. While awaiting their release, slaves were used as domestics or workers in government projects. In some cases they were permitted gainful employment in order to earn their ransom. Descendants of Tabarcans[10] enslaved in 1740 were still living in Tunis early in the 19th century, operating shops and pursuing trades. They were slaves only nominally. The less fortunate had to spend their nights in the bagnio where they were confined before sunset.

The End of Barbary Privateering

What conclusions about the function of privateering in the precolonial Maghrib does this evidence support?

Socially, privateering was marginal activity. Compared with the dense rural masses, the handful of rais, sailors, and miscellaneous beneficiaries of prize money was insignificant. Economically, privateering was equally unimportant, particularly since its achievements were so irregular. In 1812, the value of all Algerian prizes was 2,136,675 gold francs. The previous year it had amounted to only a quarter as much, while in 1813 it totalled scarcely a tenth. In some years the number of seizures was derisory. No slaves were taken in 1811, there were only four ships captured in 1801, and only one in 1803.

On the whole, profits were both mediocre and risky. The taxes on the harvests, even considering the capricious climate, undoubtedly raised surer and more substantial revenue. Rural taxes were more certain because sea battles did not always end in victory and the fighting did produce some casualties. The risks and losses in privateering cannot be measured, but the history of the corsairs is filled with them. Rais Hamidu, for example, died in an 1815 encounter with Commodore Decatur.[11]

Finally, when the commercial activity of any Christian port is compared with the corsairs' undertakings, the low level of the latter is obvious. Between 1794 and 1798, a yearly average of 225 boats originating in the Muslim Mediterranean from Greece to Morocco anchored at Livorno. At Marseille, the number of incoming ships averaged 2,400 a year. Figures for Tunis and Algiers pale by comparison with those of the major Mediterranean ports.

Christian Europe overestimated the power of the Algerian and Tunisian corsairs, just as it greatly exaggerated the misery of conditions in captivity. These misconceptions ultimately induced Europe to eliminate the corsair menace when peace returned to the Mediterranean. They were not, however, the only inducements, for the English admiral Sidney Smith raised the issue of Barbary privateering at the Congress of Vienna as much to forestall discussion of the abolition of the Knights of Malta and the island's new status as for any other reason. Besides, as the Christian shores of the Mediterranean were freed from privateering, new areas for commercial exploitation would open.

Europe's anxiety, whether more or less charitably motivated, led, in 1816, to the naval expedition of Lord Exmouth. In March, the English admiral anchored off Algiers and forced the dey to free slaves from the Ionian Islands, Sardinia, and Naples. Arriving in Tunis the next month, he met with still greater success, convincing the bey not only to free European slaves, but also to forbid the future enslavement of Christians. After sailing on to Tripoli, the admiral returned to Algiers to procure, as he had in Tunis, the definitive abolition of both Christian slavery and privateering. When the dey refused, Exmouth bombarded Algiers, forcing him to yield on the matter of emancipation for Europeans but not on the termination of privateering. In fact, the departure of the British was rapidly followed by the reorganization of the Algerian fleet. In Tunisia the Greek War served as a pretext to engage once again in privateering, but these lapses did not finally stem the irreversible decline of privateering. When Algiers fell to the French in 1830, only a few hundred slaves remained in the city.

Notes

1. The Knights of Malta were members of a religious order founded to aid pilgrims in the Holy Land. Driven from Palestine in 1291, they controlled the island of Rhodes until 1523 when the Ottomans forced them to

flee to Malta. The Order flourished there until Napoleon seized the island en route to Egypt in 1798. The Knights harassed Muslim commerce and shipping through the 16th and 17th centuries, standing firm in the face of Sulaiman the Magnificent's efforts to dislodge them in 1565. See E. W. Schermerhorn, *Malta of the Knights* (London, 1929); and Salvatore Bono, *I corsari barbareschi* (Turin, 1964), chapter 3.

2. Jacques Godechot, "La Course maltaise le long des côtes barbaresques à la fin du XVIIIe siècle," *Revue Africaine,* no. 96 (1952), pp. 105-113.

3. Quoted in Jean Mathiex, "Sur la marine marchande barbaresque," *Annales ESC,* 1958, p. 90.

4. Marcel Emerit, "L'essai d'une marine marchande barbaresque au XVIIIe siècle," *Cahiers de Tunisie,* no. 11 (1955), pp. 363-70.

5. B. Forteguerri, *O più pace, o più guerra. Memoria riguardante il sistema di pace, e di guerra che le potenze europee practicano con le reggenze di Barberia* (Naples, 1786).

6. This official was actually closer to a foreign minister than a naval official. Since the Muslim world was considered as one entity and the non-Muslim world as another, dealings with foreigners most often involved maritime contacts, thus explaining the use of this title.

7. A. Devoulx, "Le Registre des prises maritimes," *Revue Africaine,* 15 (1871), pp. 70-79, 149-160, 184-201, 285-299, 362-374, 447-457, and 16 (1872), pp. 70-77, 146-156, 233-240, 292-303.

8. On these raids, see G. Loth, "Le Pillage de Saint Pierre de Sardaigne par les corsaires tunisiens en 1798," *Revue Tunisienne,* 12 (1905), pp. 9-14, and Salvatore Bono, "L'Incursione dei corsari tunisini a Carloforte e il riscatto degli schiavi carolini (1798-1803)," *Africa,* 15 (1960), pp. 234-38.

9. The commenda was a commercial agreement developed in the Middle Ages whereby one individual gave capital or goods to a second to trade. The original investor received an amount equal to his initial investment plus a share of the profits, the remainder of which the second party retained as payment for his work.

10. Tabarca, an island off the northern coast of Tunisia, had been in Genoese hands since 1540 and was used as a base for the business of Italian merchants.

11. The United States declared war on Algiers on March 2, 1815, in an effort to end privateering raids against American vessels plying the Mediterranean. For an account of Hamidu's last battle, see Gardner W. Allen, *Our Navy and the Barbary Corsairs* (Boston, 1905; reprinted, Hamden, Connecticut, 1965), pp. 281-84.

6.
International Commerce: The Trojan Horse of the European Advance

Privateering was a lucrative undertaking for the rulers of the regencies, if not an essential part of their economies. Moreover, when Tunisia and Algeria came to terms with most of the Christian countries, the potential victims of privateering greatly declined while, at the same time, potential trading partners grew and commerce developed even with those regions which the corsairs had threatened most. Opening a window to the Muslim, and especially the Christian, worlds beyond North Africa, this trade introduced profound changes to the Maghrib, ushering in new styles, creating new demands, and ultimately precipitating a confrontation between the opposite shores of the Mediterranean.

The Range of Trade

One must first establish the geographical extent of the trade. The Maghrib had only temporary and insignificant dealings with England, Holland, Scandanavia, and other northern European areas. Since no direct trade linked North Africa with those regions, English textiles and metal products normally entered Morocco via Gibraltar and Tunisia or Algeria via Livorno. The Maghrib had even fewer business contacts with non-European countries, and only the occasional passage of American vessels acquainted it with the existence of the New World.

North Africa's trade network was confined to the Mediterranean Basin. Naturally, exchanges developed between Muslim countries and their closest neighbors, Morocco and Oran supplying wheat, poultry, and beef to Spain while Tunisia sent Malta wheat, oil, and cattle. Only in Morocco, however, did these dealings with adjacent territories assume major importance. The pivotal points for North African commerce were Marseille, Italy (especially Livorno), and the Levant (the Mediterranean coastline from Egypt to Greece).

Even within this narrowly circumscribed area, groups of merchants divided up the region. France, for example, was the preserve of the Marseille traders. Intent on preventing the creation of North African merchant fleets, they also looked askance at any Muslims and Jews adventurous enough to cross the Mediterranean. Although treaties provided reciprocal advantages for merchants, they were not warmly welcomed. In Marseille, in 1770, two Moroccans wanted to convert a pavilion inside the Muslim cemetery into a mosque to facilitate the performance of their religious duties. Christian merchants had hospices in Islamic countries, but the Chamber of Commerce nevertheless rejected the request. Whenever Jewish entrepreneurs tried to establish agents in Marseille, they encountered a multitude of hindrances designed to shorten their stay. Such harassment greeted North African traders whenever they landed at Marseille and the city's Chamber of Commerce continually pressured the Ministry of the Navy to ban their entry. In 1757, 1767, and 1773 the Marseille lobby attempted to close the port in contravention of existing treaties. The Ministry never completely yielded, but it continued to seek legal means to block North African competition.

The North Africans did not endure these obstructive policies passively. The dey issued several protests in 1775 and the merchants stubbornly persisted in their efforts to trade with the Christians, profiting by such favorable circumstances as European conflicts. The Seven Years War and the fighting of the Revolutionary and Napoleonic periods provided the Maghribi businessmen with new opportunities to install agents in Marseille. The first tentative appearance of North African trade came in 1793 when a Tunisian Jew sent a shipment. After 1795 the experiment was repeated and although Tunisian subjects probably acted as fronts for French merchants, they did share in the profits.

A quarter of the vessels loaded in Tunisia and sailing to Marseille carried cargoes belonging to Tunisians or at least so listed (see Document 13, Table 1, page 97). Some of the ships also had passports from the regency.

A few Moroccan merchants travelled to Marseille in 1813 and 1814 to sell skins, ostrich plumes, gold, cotton, and wax. Algerian Jews also became involved in this trade. Although there is limited information about the business dealings of these men, the Bakri family is sufficiently well known to verify the attempts to establish businesses of the dey's subjects in the French port.[1]

With the restoration of peace, however, the Tunisian merchants vanished almost completely. From 1815 to 1830, while commerce resumed its prewar levels, Muslim merchants dispatched only four shipments and Jewish merchants only a dozen. The North Africa-Marseille trade remained a French monopoly.

Frenchmen even controlled trade between Tunis and the Iberian Peninsula, a market particularly vital for Tunisian manufacturing since Spain provided fine wool and Portugal first class vermilion for the chechia industry. In return, Tunisia sold grain and oil to Spain. Until the Napoleonic Wars, however, these commodities moved through Marseille, which naturally raised their prices in Tunis. The Tunisians resented this inconvenience and, during the Empire, seized control of the trade from the French merchants. As in other instances, the renewal of peace ended this attempt at economic independence.

In the Tunis-Livorno trade the Jews were preeminent. Late in the 18th century, commerce was booming in the Medici port and statistics reveal that vessels from the Maghrib occupied a prominent place among ships entering Livorno from the Muslim Mediterranean (see Document 13, Table 2, page 97). In the first third of the 19th century, as trade networks changed and their volume increased, the importance of the Maghrib declined. Nevertheless, traffic between the two ports remained active and coral and tuna fishing by Italian barks reinforced commercial dealings.

Certainly the Levant trade was in the hands of North African Muslims and Jews, but that did not mean an equal division, because the carriers were again Christians. The absence of a merchant fleet compelled the North Africans to rely on Ragusan, Venetian, and French shippers. Consequently, conflicts between the Christian powers played havoc with their trade, adding to the frustration of dependence. Even during the imperial wars, when the Tunisians briefly eliminated French intermediaries, vessels plying the Levant route remained Christian.

In trade with all corners of the Mediterranean, Tunisia held a permanent superiority over Morocco and Algeria. Contemporary witnesses agreed on this and objective sources bear them out. As the historian Carmelo Trasselli put it, Tunis was the "Shanghai of the Mediterranean." From 1790 to 1799, 347 of the 749 ships (46.3 percent) entering Marseille harbor from North Africa came from Tunis. Similarly, at Livorno arrivals from Tunis exceeded those from Algiers or Morocco. In the late 18th century (1793–1798), Tunis was Livorno's major trading partner in the Muslim Mediterranean, surpassing even Smyrna, Alexandria, and Istanbul. Turning to Egypt, Pierre-Simon Girard's contributions to the *Description de l'Egypte* state that ten or twelve ships a year sailed from Alexandria to Tunis, three or four to Algiers, and two or three to Tripoli.[2] Virtually everything Egypt imported from North Africa except for the yellow leather shoes of Morocco, however, was produced in and shipped from Tunisia.

In Morocco, on the other hand, the sultan protested in 1816 that he would have "absolutely no trade. I do not wish to receive a penny from customs." The Moroccan ports dealt regularly with Lisbon, Gibraltar, and Cadiz, and only rarely with Tripoli, Tunis, and Marseille.

All signs point to the usefulness of studying the nature and volume of Tunis' trade, especially with Livorno and the Levant. As for Marseille, the existence of a special commercial organization, the Company of Africa, requires us to treat its trade in a broader context which includes Algeria.

Tunisian Commerce with Livorno and the Levant

The primary characteristic of Tunisian trade with the Levant, which also serves as a contrast to its commerce with Marseille, was the variety of cargoes, comprising consignments assembled by countless merchants, each of whom exported small quantities. A typical cargo manifest for a vessel bound from Tunis to Smyrna (see Document 14, pages 98-101) listed twenty Jewish shippers and an indeterminate number of Muslim shippers responsible for 114 crates of chechias and various other parcels.

The woolen hats of Tunis led the list of exports, followed by the white woolens of Djerba, of which Girard maintains the regency annually exported 8,000 pieces to Alexandria, and Djerban burnouses. Wax, honey, and oils also went to Alexandria, the latter being shipped in Djerban jars since casks might previously have held wine. Black slaves frequently rounded out a cargo. In sum, manufactured products and luxury items dominated this trade.

In return, Tunisia received silk and white slaves from Smyrna and Istanbul; vermilion and gall nuts from the

Morea; Cashmere linens, cloth and shawls; and linen and cotton goods, rice, raw cotton, and raw linen from Alexandria. On rare occasions, as in 1818 – 1822, when there were shortages at home, Tunisia imported grain from the Levant. Normally, however, imports consisted of heavy goods and raw materials (silk, vermilion, and linen) or expensive products of Levantine industries. There was only one partially complementary aspect of the two economies: the vermilion of the Morea and the rice of Alexandria had no equivalents in Tunisian production; the trade in cloth and slaves, on the contrary, depended on luxurious whims rather than economic imperatives.

Tunisia did not consume all these Levantine products itself. Some were transported overland to sub–Saharan Africa and eastern Algeria, adding profits derived from brokerage fees to those won in direct trade.

These qualitative facts can be strengthened by figures, the volume of traffic providing a good starting point. There is an inventory of vessels whose manifests were registered with the Venetian consul in Tunis from 1792 to 1797. The register is an especially good source since it covers a period during which the French merchant marine was inactive and also because the Venetians acted only as carriers in Tunis — there were no Venetian merchants in the regency. Of 284 sailings, 29 (10 percent) were for Egypt, Asia Minor, or Istanbul. Skipping the era of the imperial wars for which data are misleading, the years beginning with 1820 again provide accurate figures. Statistics covering all of Tunisia's commercial traffic from 1820 to 1826, with some gaps in 1823 and 1825, show 755 ships leaving Tunis for either the Levant or Europe, 126 (16 percent) for the former (see Document 13, Tables 3 and 4, page 98).

The initial data, then, suggest that commercial traffic between Tunis and the Levant did not decline at the end of the 18th century or, in spite of the Greek War, early in the 19th.

The value of exports offers another index. In 1816,

shipments to the Levant composed 12.3 percent of Tunisia's exports. By 1824, the total volume of exports had risen to 5,876,060 francs, of which chechias alone accounted for 2,253,835 francs. When wool, octopuses, and salt are added, cargoes shipped to the Levant totalled 38 percent of all exports. The balance of trade favored Tunisia, and Alexandria, Smyrna, and Istanbul sent cash to pay for their purchases.

By 1826, the picture had changed. Tunisian exports exceeded eight million francs in value, but manufactured products shipped to the Levant were worth only 987,000 francs, or 11.7 percent of exports.

Although certainly fragmentary evidence, these figures do give an indication of relative importance which is confirmed by observations made in Alexandria. As late as 1836, Egyptian trade with North Africa represented, in value, 6.7 percent of its imports. The Maghrib ranked seventh in Alexandrian exports but held sixth place in that city's imports, the balance favoring the Maghrib.

Thirty years later, Tunisia supplied a mere one percent of Egypt's imports; the rupture of the traditional commercial links had been completed. Nevertheless, in terms of the late 18th and early 19th centuries, a regular and lucrative, if not large, commerce linked the Maghrib, and especially Tunisia, with the rest of the Muslim Mediterranean, providing one element in North Africa's economic equilibrium.

At first sight, Tunisian trade with Livorno was quite similar to that with the Levant. It was marked by mixed cargoes in baskets, sacks, and bales; by countless shipping agents, each providing only a small portion of the freight; and by a tendency to export finished products. Fernand Braudel and Ruggiero Romano, in their analysis of Livornese commerce in the 16th century, noted the absence of specialization among the Tuscan merchants who "engaged in every kind of commerce, shipping to various regions at the same time."[3] The trade of Livorno seems to have been much the same at the end of the 18th century. Moreover, goods coming from Tunis early in the 17th century were the same as two centuries later, including wool, leather, wax, dates, oil, and fabrics.

In reality, however, Livorno's trade certainly had an ambivalent character. Socially, for example, although there was a multitude of merchants involved in the export business and although a familial business structure can be detected — such names as Lumbroso, Valensi, and Costa constantly reappear on the manifests decade after decade — a more modern structure was juxtaposed to the traditional one. The Livornese merchants of Tunis constituted a company called *"de la journée."* Tax farmers for the regency's leather, they held a monopoly on all hides sold, and exported them to Italy.

Other important exports were heifer and cow hides and jackal and camel skins. While rarely constituting complete cargoes, grains and other foodstuffs did assume a significant place in the shipments. For example, 86 percent of the vessels arriving in Livorno from Tunis between 1794 and 1798 carried some grain in their cargo. After the wars, Europe imported grain from Odessa, but by that time, except for the years 1824 and 1826, Tunisia was no longer in a position to export its grain. Wheat was replaced by a new agricultural product, olive oil. In the 1820s, 20 percent of the ships coming from Tunis were transporting it.

The addition of dates, olives, wax, and wool to the list of exports makes it clear that unprocessed or raw materials composed more of Tunisia's exports to Italy than did manufactured goods. Before 1830, however, commercial specialization was not the rule, and shawls, woolen covers, rose water, soap, and chechias were still regularly exported. Tunis also retained its role as intermediary between Africa and Italy, sending ostrich plumes, elephant tusks, and senna across the Mediterranean during the first third of the 19th century.

Imports from Livorno paralleled those from Marseille, both in their nature and in the changes in them after 1815.

Livorno acted mainly as an entrepôt, redistributing products imported from elsewhere in Europe and the colonies. The important wool of Segovia, sugar, coffee, all kinds of spices, such industrial products of central Europe and England as cloth and hardware, and Venetian paper and glass were among the commodities shipped to North Africa. Livorno supplied Tunisia with these goods even after 1815 although by then English calico and cloth had become principal items among the exports. Similar changes occurred in Algeria and Morocco, where Jewish merchants imported English fabrics and hardware from Gibraltar.

It is impossible to determine whether this trans-Mediterranean commerce favored the Maghrib or Livorno and Gibraltar, but two facts about it are very important. First, the invasion of European industrial products had the twofold effect of competing with local industry and draining off currency. Secondly, during the 18th century and the early years of the 19th, Tunisian and Algerian consignments to Livorno invariably included *groups,* or small sealed packets holding a wide variety of coins and bars of precious metals. Since the exporting of these *groups* cannot be measured, it would be rash to assert that there was a flight of coin. One certain fact is that profits which the Tuscan merchants earned in this trade were sent to Italy and invested there, not in the Maghrib.

Marseille and the Maghrib: A Trade Economy

Between Marseille and the Regency of Algiers, the Company of Africa, created by royal edict in 1741 and headquartered in the southern French port, controlled trade. Since the loss of Cape Negre in 1741, the Company did not have a secure trading post in Tunisia, although a treaty signed in 1748 and renewed on several occasions did grant it a monopoly of coral fishing. This arrangement brought the bey some revenue, but it had no impact on the regency's internal economy. In Algeria, on the other hand, the Company had warehouses in Bône and Collo and a large settlement at La Calle which, by 1789, had become a community populated by Frenchmen. The Company held the coral monopoly there, but its chief purpose was buying wheat and hides in eastern Algeria.

Just before the French Revolution, the trade prospered. Of all the companies created by the Ancien Régime, only the Company of Africa avoided deficits and distributed dividends to its shareholders. Algeria also profited from its dealings with the Company since wheat was purchased only with cash, and usually with Spanish piasters which, everywhere in the Maghrib, were always the preferred, and sometimes the only acceptable, currency in the Ancien Régime. The rate of the piaster was artificially high in North Africa and to complicate matters the practice of clipping piasters continued until 1792. Eastern Algeria did not, however, import European products.

Even the capital's imports did not balance these exports. In terms of value, Marseille merchants sent far less to Algeria than they received, and a single firm sufficed to handle the limited transactions.

Altogether, the sale of Algerian products in France was a lucrative business for the Company, although the balance of payments favored the regency.

The Revolution and the turmoil of the Empire seriously affected commerce, although the Company did not go out of business. In spite of the suppression of monopolies, the need for adequate grain supplies prompted the revolutionary government to retain the former royal company under the new title of the Africa Agency. Until 1799 this Agency was able to buy wheat in Algeria, but thereafter changes in political relations between the two countries, the dealings of the Bakri family, who had agents in both Marseille and Paris by the late 1790s, and the shortage of Spanish piasters all combined to hinder a restoration of the company's former prosperity.

After the Restoration, Algeria granted France some of

the privileges enjoyed by the old Company, but France declined to create a new agency. The Marseille mercantile firm of Paret was the holder of the new concessions in Algiers, but the trade declined and in a short time only one or two ships a year were arriving from Marseille. In Tunis, in the meantime, commerce with France was very simple. Cargoes tended to be uniform, vessels carrying only wheat from the northern coast or oil and wool from the Sahel. Merchants even specialized, each loading an entire boat and regularly making shipments to the Marseille businessmen whose agents they were. Of all the North African ports, only Tunis bears comparison with those of the Levant. French merchants lived in their own "community," governed and protected by their consul. Until the late 18th century, their numbers, business conduct, and even private lives were rigorously controlled. Later they had greater freedom, but the number of French houses involved in the Tunisian trade remained small enough to allow each to make a profit. Frenchmen had a business advantage in that they paid only a 5 percent import tax, whereas Jews paid an 11 percent ad valorem tax.

Relations between Tunisia and France changed after the French Revolution, as had Franco-Algerian relations. In peacetime, however, French merchants resumed their previous position by developing a new branch of the Tunisian economy, the export of olive oil.

For all practical purposes, Marseille's exports to Tunis in the closing years of the Ancien Régime duplicated those of Livorno, except for fabrics which came in small quantities from Languedoc. Marseille, in turn, imported such Tunisian agricultural products as hides, wool, and wax, but the grain trade was the mainstay of French commerce. Half the French ships loaded in Tunis from 1781 to 1793 carried grain, and statistics published by Ruggiero Romano indicate that 14 percent to 34 percent of the wheat entering Marseille in the 1780s came from North Africa.[4] Overall, the value of the products which Tunisia imported was less than that of goods sent to Marseille, resulting in French cash payments to

Tunisia as well as Algeria.

TABLE I
Entries To Marseille Of Ships From Tunisia

	Total Number	Carrying Wheat (%)	Carrying Oil (%)
1800-1809	262	21.3	62.9
1810-1819	206	17	65.5
1820-1829	555	4	78.4

This situation reversed itself after the Empire. As textiles and other industrial products assumed primacy among imports, Tunisian customers were unable to pay cash for their acquisitions, and French merchants made profits of 100 percent or 200 percent. Oil became the major export, sometimes representing almost all French imports from Tunisia in terms of value.

In the prerevolutionary era, the wheat trade did not affect prices and had even less impact on social conditions for the peasantry in the regency. The bey, who sold export authorizations (tadhkira*) profited from it, but it remained of only marginal importance for the regency's economy. The same did not apply to the oil trade, which did influence the social equilibrium of producing regions.

The reasons for this were complex. Since the maritime wars and especially since the banning of privateering, the bey had sought new revenue in commerce. Towards this end, he assumed for himself a monopoly of the sale of oil to foreign merchants, disposing of it at twice the price he had paid his subjects. The businessmen remained unhurt, however, because the bey offset their increased costs by eliminating the charge for tadhkiras. Even this 100 percent profit did not suffice to balance Tunisia's flagging finances, and the ruler resorted to another new practice, the advance sale of oil at an extremely low price, in 1827. This practice involved obvious risks, since a failed harvest could result in unhonored commitments. This happened at the end of 1828 when it became apparent that there would be no crop.

The French merchants forced the bey to agree to a ruinous arrangement and to repurchase all the oil sold to them in advance. The initial purchase rate had been seven piasters per métal*, but the repurchase rate was based on oil prices in Marseille, which were twelve piasters per métal. In essence, the bey paid 71 percent interest on money advanced to him by the foreigners.

Moreover, once embarked on this decline, Tunisia was unable to free herself from the merchants' grasp. With no harvest, French businessmen had no outlets for their capital, prompting them to turn to usury and pawnbroking at monthly interest rates of one percent. Some of their clients were even members of the bey's entourage, and the ruler's financial problems steadily worsened. Moreover, the bey subjected oil producers to more and more intense pressures. For example, in addition to the tenth of the harvest he customarily received as a tithe, he appropriated oil intended for sale or export, of which he already had the monopoly. Needless to say, the price paid to his subjects was poor. Borrowing the methods of European merchants, the sovereign even paid advances against the harvest to the peasants, resulting in a further lowering of the purchase price of oil. If the harvest did not meet the grower's expectations, he had no choice but to mortgage subsequent harvests. Finally, in the wake of the disastrous 1828 accord, the bey attempted to recoup from his subjects the losses he had sustained at the hands of the French by demanding, for several years, deliveries of oil in payment of the advances made in 1828.

The treaty of 1830, which coincided with the capture of Algiers, terminated the bey's monopoly, but placed the Sahel fellah completely at the mercy of foreign merchants.

The lack of merchant vessels, the termination of privateering, the aggressive reappearance of European merchants after the peace settlements, and the creation of a trade economy which rapidly provoked a social malaise were all factors combining to contribute to a crisis in the North African economy which, year in and year out, had satisfied the modest needs of the population. Morocco had thus far avoided contamination, but its "opening" was not far off. In 1830, to revive an economy encumbered with debts accumulated when it had been necessary to import wheat in 1825-1826, Moulay ʿAbd al-Rahman opened his ports to European trade, exporting cereals collected as tax payments. The wheat trade was soon organized at Larache, Mazagan, and Casablanca.

The modification of the Levantine commercial circuits, coupled with the competition of European industries, soon created additional difficulties for North Africa's urban economy. Since the battle was not between equals, it resulted in the subordination of North Africa to an advanced and advancing Europe.

Notes

1. The Bakris, along with their Algerian Jewish associates, the Bushnaqs, engaged in extensive trans-Mediterranean trade in the closing decades of the 18th century. Accumulated French debts to these merchants precipitated the infamous "fly-whisk" or "coup d'éventail" incident in 1827 which ended in the French occupation of Algiers three years later. See Charles-André Julien, *Histoire de l'Algérie contemporaine, conquête et colonisation* (Paris, 1964), particularly chapter 1 and its bibliography.

2. The *Description* was a massive work prepared by scholars and scientists who had accompanied Napoleon's expedition to Egypt in 1798. It covered a wide range of topics, including commercial statistics.

3. Fernand Braudel and Ruggiero Romano, *Navires et marchandise à l'entrée du port de Livourne, 1547-1611* (Paris, 1951), p. 75.

4. Ruggiero Romano, *Commerce et prix du blé à Marseille au XVIIIe siècle* (Paris, 1956).

7.
The Maghrib in
the Muslim Community

The North Africans were ill-prepared for this political subordination. Their world view prior to the French conquest
hinged on two concepts: the existence of certain political and
cultural spheres to which North Africa belonged and the
existence of an alien region confronting these spheres, the
Bar al-Nasara or continent of the Christians.

Questions about the nature of the North African states,
the accuracy of referring to them as "nations" before the
conquest, and the relationship between the center and the
periphery, elude decisive answers, in part due to the heated
debates these issues have recently stimulated (see Appendix
2, pages 111-120), but also because matters concerning collective consciousness are extremely difficult to define.

From Elective Monarchy to Military Republic

In precolonial North Africa there were three separate states.
The Maghrib was not a monolithic political unit, nor were
relations between its component governments continuous or
even necessarily friendly. For instance, Sultan Moulay

71

Slimane used the Darqawa Brotherhood to support a revolt against the Turks in Oran; and the government of Tunis, under Algerian control since 1756, terminated a humiliating, if not onerous, guardianship when Hammuda Pasha refused to send the annual tribute, rebuilt frontier fortifications, and launched a victorious campaign in 1807. Peace returned to the regencies only in 1821, however, and even then only through Ottoman mediation.[1]

These clearly separate and autonomous political entities held sway over fixed territories and were acknowledged by the population, although not in the sense of individuals expressing "national" sentiments. Rather, every North African, whether urban or rural, considered himself a subject of one of the rulers. Revolts were actually challenges to authority, not indications of anarchy.

An examination of the operation of each state and of relations between rulers and ruled enhances the understanding of the precolonial Maghrib. The Moroccan monarchy unquestionably conformed to the social structures previously described better than the other systems. In the first place, the monarchy rested on a genealogy traceable to the Prophet and established as clearly as that of any important tribe, as is apparent from the genealogy's transcription by Ali al-Abbassi.[2] Moreover, in spite of the hereditary nature of the monarchy it was, in reality, elective, in line with traditions already discussed. The sultan needed the recognition of the major cities, the tribes, and the army, just as tribal chiefs owed their positions to selection by their subordinates rather than to the use of force (see Document 15, page 101).

This selection process invited dissidence, since failure to agree on a candidate resulted in another member of the family presenting his candidacy in opposition. When Moulay Yazid died in 1792, the south proclaimed Moulay 'Abd al-Rahman sultan, while Marrakesh acknowledged Moulay Hisham, his brother, and Moulay Maslama attracted followers in the north. Moulay Slimane, who emerged triumphant from these struggles and ruled until 1822, initially had support only from the city of Fez, the 'abid corps, the white guard, and the Berbers. It took him four years to establish his supremacy and he entered Marrakesh only in 1796. Dynastic loyalty never wavered during this long succession crisis, but local and regional antipathies did crystallize over the choice of a sovereign.

Social life, including education, justice, and religion, was the concern of the tribe, village, guild, or ethnic group. This structure greatly simplified the duties of the state, reducing them to raising taxes and maintaining public security. The ruler could build and support mosques and madrasas*, particularly in the cities. The sultan did, admittedly, have some responsibility for public welfare, in fulfilment of which he opened the state granaries when famine threatened, but such duties did not burden the state's budget.

This distribution of responsibilities had two results. First, there was almost no administrative apparatus — no salaried functionaries and no centralized administration whose employees were named by the government. The men around the sultan were servants rather than ministers, while governors who saw to the policing of the roads and markets, the collection of taxes, and the overall provision of public tranquillity were all that was needed in the provinces.

Secondly, the limited nature of the state sometimes caused its citizens to lose sight of its necessity. Revolts, which were refusals to pay taxes above all else, were a constant factor in Morocco's internal affairs. The sultan had three mechanisms for containing centrifugal forces: the reinforcement of the army; the military conquest of the rebels, either by using loyal tribes or by dividing the resisters; and the introduction of the makhzan's agents or the recognition of those local chiefs who, ignoring the tribal councils' authority, were prepared to deliver the population under their control to the central government. Moulay Slimane's successors, especially Moulay Hassan, took the latter approach, but Moulay Slimane devoted much of his long reign to suppressing revolts. In addition to his early difficulties in gaining recognition, he waged campaigns in the Draa (1802), the Rif (1803), and the regions of Taza and Oudjda (1804). After 1811, bloody revolts swept through the Middle Atlas and the Berbers briefly captured the sultan, who owed his safety only to the respect due to sharifs. Nevertheless, his prestige was permanently damaged by this incident. Near the end of his reign the cities, the Black guards, and the Oudaya, or white guards, all revolted, each proclaiming a new sultan. Lacking financial resources, Moulay Slimane, more a scholar than a soldier, and poorly supported by his small and undisciplined armed forces, failed to establish the makhzan's hold over the whole country.

The system of choosing the ruler in Algiers differed considerably, although the functions of the state and the style of its relations with its subjects did not. Only Turks of the Algiers militia participated in the choice of a sovereign, the hinterlands playing no part in the palace coups which brought most reigns to tragic ends. Until 1816, the dey was a virtual prisoner of the militia. Once elected, he was taken from his family which he then saw only twice a week. In 1816, Ali Khodja barricaded himself in the Qasba*, brought his harem there, and freed himself from the janissaries*.

The sultan did not share power in Morocco, but in Algiers a number of people in the odjak* helped govern the regency, including the khaznadar* or treasurer; the wakil al-kharidj, or foreign affairs minister; and officers of the bait al-mal* which retained possession of estates for whom there were no heirs. In any case, the size of the country dictated its division into provinces in which executive power rested with beys, while the dey directly governed the suburbs of Algiers and the Mitidja Plain, the Dar al-Sultan. The bey of Titeri controlled the center of the regency, and the bey of Constantine presided over the east, while the bey of Oran ruled in the west after the Spanish evacuation in 1792. Once an individual attained the office of bey, normally by offering more money for it than his rivals, he was required only to remit tax money to Algiers twice yearly and to go to the capital in person every third year. The beys never established dynasties as did their namesakes in Tunis. The dey appointed them and from 1790 to 1825 eight were relieved and another sixteen executed, from which one may judge their dependence on the central government.

Thus, in both Algiers and the provinces, power rested unsteadily on a constantly renewed caste of Turks recruited in the Levant. Beneath this turbulence, however, the people remained more or less autonomous, just as in Morocco and Tunisia. This was true whether qaids, who were generally Turks, governed rural areas by relying on Turkish garrisons and naming shaikhs chosen by the villagers, or whether the tribes and brotherhoods administered themselves semi-independently of any central authority, as did the Muqranis in the Medjana or the Awlad Sidi Shaikh in the Oranais. Consequently, the contacts between the overwhelmingly rural Algerian population and the dey or the provincial beys were not essentially different from those between the Moroccan monarch and his subjects. It is an exaggeration to describe Algeria as a colonial state fleeced by a foreign ruling class. The tax structure was similar throughout the Maghrib, and armed forces were weak everywhere and relied on help from auxiliary tribes to collect taxes and maintain order.

It is worth noting, as many other historians have done, that even with limited means — little centralization, small administrations, and few troops — the Turkish government provided a measure of public tranquillity which eluded the later colonial regime. It is true, however, that on the eve of the conquest, revolts in the west aided by the Darqawa Brotherhood and others in the east seriously impaired the authority of the dey and the entire Turkish administration.

In Tunis, as in Algiers, the militia was recruited in the Levant until 1811. It was just as insolent as the Algiers militia, and its lack of discipline erupted into public disorders in 1811, 1816, and 1829. These outbursts were not, however, critical. In 1705 a dynasty which retained power until the postindependence proclamation of the Tunisian republic established itself. Although the dynasty's founder was a descendant of a Turk from Candia, it had no ties with the Ottoman Empire and few in the court spoke Turkish. This family, the Hussainids, provided all the subsequent beys, although there were occasional succession crises, most notably in 1814.

Tunisia's urban culture, the presence of an artisanal and commercial bourgeoisie, and the relatively large number of educated individuals created conditions favoring the recruitment of administrative personnel — a vastly different situation from that in Algeria. Renegades and white slaves from the Levant did hold positions of prestige in the bey's entourage, but native Tunisians also shared in power. Their ranks often supplied the qaids, as illustrated by the Djellouli dynasty in Sfax and the Sahel. Moreover, the country's small size and physical structure, coupled with the dense sedentarization of many areas, enabled the administration to control its subjects more effectively than the neighboring countries could.

Tunisian dealings with other Mediterranean states and the needs of commerce also encouraged the beys to pursue policies quite different from those of other North African rulers. The personality of Hammuda Pasha played a decisive role in formulating these attitudes. The most enlightened of his line, Hammuda used the European wars as a pretext to reinforce his army and navy without offending the dey. He then declared his independence from Algiers. When the Turks revolted, he simply dissolved the militia, replacing it with local recruits. The disruption of commerce by the wars gave Hammuda the opportunity, which he seized, to deprive French merchants of their control over Tunisia's trade, allowing key aspects of commerce to accumulate in the hands of his own retainers. He revised customs tariffs, which, in spite of rising prices, had not been updated since 1753, and made improvements to the port of Tunis. To foster local industry, he set an example for his people by forsaking luxury clothes from the East and wearing instead cloth woven at

Djerba. A coherent and sustained policy, aimed at strengthening the bey's power and independence, augmenting the resources of his treasury, and promoting Tunisian business, gave Hammuda's government a distinctive style. The dey of Algiers was a janissary, the first soldier of the kingdom, a "primus inter pares," but the bey of Tunis was much more, and state and society were better integrated in Hammuda's reign than they were in Algeria.

This was a fragile equilibrium, however. The end of privateering and the concomitant reduction of revenues, the resurgence of foreign merchants and European products, and economic difficulties connected with bad harvests or epidemics resulted in a financial crisis for the state which, in turn, aggravated the tax burden on the people.

The Ottoman Empire and the Community of Believers

Another political entity which encompassed only a part of the Maghrib was the Ottoman Empire, of which Algeria and Tunisia were provinces. The suzerainty of the Porte was, from a political and diplomatic standpoint, a fiction. In Algiers a diwan*, or superior council, composed of officers and high officials, elected the dey, while in Tunisia the Hussainid family provided the beys. The Ottoman sultan had no part in the selection of the rulers except to accord them investiture firmans* at their accession and annual firmans of confirmation thereafter.

Neither Algiers nor Tunis sent tribute to the Porte, the sultan had no agents in the Maghrib, and the only representatives of the regencies in Istanbul were recruiters who collected troops in the capital, Smyrna, and Anatolia, but who did not serve as consuls.

In diplomatic matters, both rulers freely signed treaties with the Christian powers. When the Porte insisted on a break in Franco-Algerian relations in 1799, the dey complied only reluctantly.

The theoretical vassalage of the regencies was not totally meaningless, however, finding expression in the send-ing of official missions, gifts, and military aid. The Ottomans requested troops in 1795 to use against Tripolitania, in 1810 for the fighting in Crete, and again during the Greek rebel-lion. On the other hand, since the sultan was the Prophet's successor, he served as supreme arbiter. Money minted in Tunis bore his seal and the Friday khutba* was given in his name. The Hanafite mufti*, appointed from Istanbul, was the head of Islam in Algeria.

In cases of acute danger, the North Africans turned to Istanbul. The last letter of the dey of Algiers was an urgent appeal for military aid from the Porte, and Tunisian tribes resisting the French occupation half a century later placed their last hopes in the arrival of Turkish reinforcements.

These pretenses of political allegiance were, however, less important than the Maghrib's involvement in the Muslim community centered on Mecca. Not only was that city the direction towards which Muslims turned in prayer, it was also Islam's birthplace and the place which many tribes claimed as their origin. Chenier remarked:

> When a Moor, on his return from Mecca, re-enters the city in which he dwells, preceded by drums and haut-boys and followed by relations and friends, he bestows a holy embrace on all he meets; and though before he was held an ignorant vagabond, he assumes on this day a hypocritical gravity which imposes on people eager to see and believe in wonders and who crowd to be hugged by him and receive an infusion of his virtue.[3]

Pejorative connotations aside, these observations are important. Other facts (the thousands of North African pil-grims from all walks of life who made the annual trip; the popularity of travel narratives, or rihla*, and the cultural contacts which the pilgrims experienced) attest to this fervor and to the psychological importance of these exchanges. "A meeting of intellectuals from all over the Muslim world," the pilgrimage to the Holy City was, as André Raymond has written, "a world congress of Islamic thought."[4]

At the same time Cairo, a stopover on the pilgrimage route, was Islam's intellectual capital. The North African scholar Muhammad al-Fassi al-Tawdi, passing through Cairo on pilgrimage in 1767-68 and 1768-69, taught courses at the al-Azhar Mosque University. Many Maghribi pilgrims spent their time in Cairo searching for rare manuscripts to bring back to their countries. The most refined North Africans completed their education there. At al-Azhar, the North African riwaq* (literally, the interval between two columns and, by extension, at al-Azhar a residence for students from the same geographic region) was one of the most numerous, liveliest, and most turbulent. In 1787, along with the Syrian students, the North Africans rose against their shaikh, took him prisoner, occupied the mosque, and forced merchants to close their shops. The founders of the popular Rahmaniyya and Tijaniyya Brotherhoods studied in Cairo, where the Halwatiyya and Hafnawiyya were counterparts of the Maghribi orders — another example of the connection between Egypt and the Maghrib.

Constant exchanges of men and ideas linked the Maghrib with the Middle East, and North African Muslims felt the solidarity within the Islamic framework more fully and deeply than any other. When they travelled in the East, they were indiscriminately referred to as Maghribis, but a reading of the Tunisian chronicle of Maqdish reveals the use of a single term to designate the inhabitants of the regency — Muslims. Sentiments associated with diverse geographic origins were superseded by sentiments of adhesion to the vast community of believers.

The Maghrib Without Europe

Although some treaties and conventions existed between the three countries and most of the Christian powers, the Maghrib thought of itself as a frontier area of Islam. Algiers was called the "bulwark of the holy war" and Tunis the "well-guarded city of the holy war." When Christian fleets appeared, Moroccan tribesmen rushed to the coast to drive off the infidels. In Sfax, in 1785, the approach of the Venetian fleet turned the entire city into an immense mosque. In Algiers, "whenever the marabouts preached the holy war or there was fear of a Christian invasion, all Kabylia united into a single soff," wrote Daumas in 1847.[5]

This state of alert was most acute on Fridays when activity within the cities ceased, for popular belief among the city people held that "the city will be taken by the Christians on a Friday."[6]

All these facts indicate that, contrary to the opinions of most contemporaries, the two societies were not prepared to listen to each other. A "coup d'éventail" precipitated the conquest of the one by the other.

On one side was an aggressive, dynamic, insatiable Europe whose history is much better known. The motives and circumstances of its expansion are familiar and need not be repeated.

On the other, North Africa was neither barbarous nor uncultured. On the contrary, careful study reveals a perfect coherence between the spiritual, economic, and social aspects of its culture. That culture was, however, different from Europe's, particularly in that nothing arose within it to stimulate the society as a whole. Its population growth was too late and too abrupt; there was not enough vitality in urban crafts or foreign commerce; and there was no intellectual renewal. The Maghrib lived at a slower pace, and this no doubt was one of the reasons for its colonization yesterday and its underdevelopment today.

Notes

See Charles-André Julien, *History of North Africa* (London, 1969), pp. 330-32.

2. Badia y Leblich, *Travels of Ali Bey,* vol. 1, p. 200.

3. L. Chenier, *Recherches historiques sur les Maures et l'histoire du Maroc,* 3 vols. (Paris, 1787). The English translation is *The Present State of the Empire of Morocco* (reprinted, New York, 1967), 1, pp. 191-2.

4. André Raymond, "Tunisiens et Maghrébins au Caire au XVIIIe siècle," *Cahiers de Tunisie,* nos. 26-27, (1959), pp. 335-71.

5. Eugène Daumas and Paul Fabar, *Etudes historiques sur la Grande Kabylie* (Paris, 1847).

6. Shaler, *Sketches.*

Appendix 1

Appendix 1

DOCUMENTS:

THE OPINIONS OF CONTEMPORARIES

DOCUMENT 1

Accepted Opinions on the Maghrib

We embarked on a galley, gilded like the altar of St. Peter's at Rome. A Sallee pirate swooped down and boarded us; our soldiers defended us like soldiers of the Pope; they threw down their arms, fell on their knees and asked the pirates for absolution *in articulo mortis.*

They were immediately stripped as naked as monkeys and my mother, our ladies of honor and myself as well . . . .

I will not tell you how hard it is for a young princess to be taken with her mother as a slave to Morocco; you will also guess all we had to endure in the pirates' ship. My mother was still very beautiful; our ladies of honor, even our waiting-maids possessed more charms than could be found in all Africa; and I was ravishing, I was beauty, grace itself, and I was a virgin; I did not remain so long; the flower which had been reserved for the handsome prince of Massa-Carrara was ravished from me by a pirate captain; he was an abominable Negro who thought he was doing me a great honor. . . .

Morocco was swimming in blood when we arrived. The fifty sons of the Emperor Moulay Ismael had each a faction; and this produced fifty civil wars, of blacks against blacks, browns against browns, mulattoes against mulattoes. There was continual carnage throughout the whole extent of the empire.

(Voltaire, *Candide*, 1759.)

DOCUMENT 2

"Barbary"

Barbary: *Barbaria,* a large district of Africa. Located between the Atlantic Ocean, the Mediterranean Sea, Egypt, and the Black lands of Guinea. Its length from east to west is considerable. The people of Barbary are devout and warlike Mohammedans. The women are very modest. In general, the coasts of Barbary are abundantly stocked with many agricultural products. The great number of seaports there facilitate commerce. Ostrich plumes, indigo, gold dust, leather, wax, tin, coral, and many fine horses are the major exports of the region.

Morocco: There are 100,000 families scattered in many *adouards* (movable villages transported from place to place by camels). Aside from these *adouards* there are many more civilized, but also more vicious, people.

(*Dictionnaire géographique,* Lyon, 1806).

DOCUMENT 3

The Base Nature of the Moors

To think justly and with candor of the Moorish character, we must take into our consideration the natural effects of a total want of education, a most rigidly arbitrary government, and a climate calculated, as far as climate has influence, to stimulate and excite the vicious passions, as well as by its debilitating and relaxing influence to weaken and depress the nobler energies of the mind. To these we may add the disadvantages arising from the want of a free intercourse with other nations, and the influence of an absurd and uncharitable religion.

(William Lemprière, *A Tour from Gibraltar to Tangier, Sallee, Mogodore, Santa Cruz, Tarudant; and thence over Mount Atlas to Morocco: Including a Particular Account of the Royal Harem etc.,* 1793, p. 291.)

DOCUMENT 4

Carthage Must Be Destroyed

In whatever light the Regency of Algiers is regarded, it would seem that one should adhere to the cry of the ancient Romans: Delenda est Carthago!

(Memoir on Algiers by the consul de Kercy, 1791. Published by Gabriel Esquer, *Reconnaissance des villes, forts, et batteries d'Alger par le chef de bataillon Boutin (1808) suivie des Mémoires sur Alger par les consuls de Kercy (1791) et Dubois-Thainville (1809),* Algiers, 1927.)

DOCUMENT 5

The State of Nature

The inclination of civilized people to be active and creative encourages constant invention and improvement. It embellishes man's home and converts Nature's products to his use. These conveniences and comforts of society, while highly laudable, are, at the same time, the bonds which make man the slave of countless artificial needs and render him unhappy if neither wealth nor work suffice to meet his needs. Accustomed from infancy to enjoy such advantages, we come to consider them so essential that we forget the toil, fatigue, and unrest which their procurement demands. We sap our strength, destroy our health, and sacrifice all our energy to acquire a fortune which often eludes us. Then, at the very edge of the grave, we again consider noble undertakings in the hopes of the so-called happiness of which death deprives us. Born amid these prejudices, I had believed in them until recently, pitying those benighted people who were unfamiliar with our fine discoveries, who had no bread, no beds, and no houses. It was hard enough for me to believe in their existence, much less imagine that such a life style was possible for a European.

Experience has opened my eyes, my dear doctor. Not only am I becoming acquainted with those men whom I believed so unhappy, I am even living among them — living as they live. I have adopted their customs, first out of necessity, but now by choice. They do not eat bread; they do not know how to prepare meats; water is their only drink. What happens as a result? They are healthier and more robust, with sickness rare among them. They have no houses, but what is the need of them in these pleasant regions where a simple tent, a hut made of foliage, or the hollow of a rock is enough, even in the worst times, to protect one from the elements? They sleep in their clothes on the ground, which is often quite damp. Does it not seem they must be plagued by the host of maladies against which medicine arms anyone foolhardy enough to do such a thing in our land? I admit to you, my dear doctor, that I was a bit frightened when it was first necessary for me to sleep in the Moorish fashion. I was, however, overwhelmed by fatigue, which proved an excellent soporific. I slept rather well, but when I awoke and felt the dampness of my clothes, I feared for my health. Happily, I suffered only slightly crushed ribs, which was nothing, and my ribs grew accustomed to the bed of the hard earth while my head adjusted to the pillow of my horse's saddle. I can assure you, my dear doctor, that with practice one sleeps as well in this way as one does in a bed enclosed in double curtains. Sleep never exceeds the requirements of Nature and causes the balm of good health to flow through the whole body. The respiration is more lively and one feels animated by a new life which one would not want to risk losing in an overly prolonged sleep.

(Abbé Poiret, *Voyage en Barbarie, ou Lettres écrites de l'Ancienne Numidie pendant les années 1785 et 1786.* 2 vols., Paris, 1789.)

DOCUMENT 6

The Spread of an Epidemic: The Algiers Plague of 1787

January 26. Many sudden deaths, with numerous fatalities in Algiers and its suburbs; it is reported that many Kabyles are dying in the countryside and that the cows and sheep suffer the same fate as the shepherds.

January 26. An ape from the Galères prison, which a number of persons had petted, contracted the plague. Seeing the animal shivering, his master took him into his bed to warm him. Both died with the swelling characteristic of the plague. A slave who made a purse from the monkey's skin also died shortly afterwards.

January 30. Until today, few Jews have died. Their leaders have issued a proclamation forbidding the purchase of clothes. They are being very careful. In January, 21 Christians, 4 Jews, and 314 Muslims died.

February 11. When the plague broke out, the Jews rushed to marry their eligible women since it is, in their view, a great sin to allow families to die out. Of the 400 people married at the time of the plague, not ten of them survive.

March 6, 1787. The plague is beginning to spread among the Jews. Despite the proscriptions of their leaders, low prices have tempted them to purchase some personal effects and used goods. They could not avoid infection by the plague, for it entered their homes by another means as well. The Moors, seeing that few Jews were dying, diverted the water which was used to wash the bodies of plague victims into their homes.

During the plague the Jews did not assemble to weep over their dead, saying that such weeping encouraged the plague — thus a mistaken conviction takes the place of a good law of health — but they did not fail to wash the corpses: 1) in cold water; 2) in boiling water with aromatic herbs.

March 12. The surgeon of the hospital (D. Sanchez) informs us that the sickness is abating into a putrid fever without swelling or carbuncles. He hopes to find some effective remedy. What he has done is leave the sick to die without interfering with nature. The swelling and the carbuncles soon reappeared with fury and almost all the Mzabites working in the public baths have died . . . .

A view of the plague compiled from details set forth in the register of Bithimel, who received a fee for every death because of the stretcher which he provided to carry the body to the grave:

First Year (1786)

Unmarried girls	1731
Boys	1571
Married and widowed white women	994
Married men and widowers	1166
Unmarried young black men and women	216
Black men and women	211
Total	5889

Second Year (1787)

Young girls	1533
Boys	730
White women	2721
Married men	2111
Black youths	46
Married black men and women	311
Total	7452

Third Year (1788)

Total	2867
GRAND TOTAL	16,208

(M. Conor, "Une épidémie de peste en Afrique mineure (1784–88) d'après le Journal des pestes, mss. du Père Vicherat, prêtre de la Mission," in *Archives de l'Institut Pasteur de Tunis*, 1911, fascicule 3, pp. 220-241.)

DOCUMENT 7

The 1818 Tangiers Plague: Death Statistics

First Phase: Outbreak

May 25–June 30, 1818	31
July	113
August	168
Total	312

Second Phase: Climax

September	267
October	479
November 1-10	216
November 11-20	189
November 21-30	171
Total	1322

Third Phase: Decline

December	328
January 1819	96
February	44
Total	468

Fourth Phase: Extinction

March	42
April	17
May 1-13	3
Total	62

Second Epidemic, or the Tail

May 22-June 30, 1819	31
July	10
August 1-11	2
Total	43

23 Jews and 4 Christians died of other illnesses
GRAND TOTAL   2,234
The population of the city was estimated at 10,640 before the
plague, meaning it killed 21 percent of the inhabitants.

(Gråberg di Hemso, *Lettera del Signor Gråberg di
Hemso al Signor Luigi Grossi sulla peste di Tangeri negli
anni 1818–1819*, Genoa and Tangiers, 1820.)

DOCUMENT 8

In the Beginning Was an Ancestor:
The Myth of the Origin of
The Walad Bou Ghanem in Tunisia

The Walad Bou Ghanem are descendants of Si Bou Ghanem,
whose shrine is on the tribe's land. Si Bou Ghanem, a direct
descendant of the prophet, came from Séguia al-Hamra in
Morocco. This is his story, pieced together in 1885:
    "Legend has it that he came alone and lived first in the
Jebel Bou Ghanem, near Foussana, which was then the seat
of a prince named Yaqub . . . .
    Once settled on the mountain, Bou Ghanem devoted
himself to prayer and each day a she-camel from Yaqub's
herd came to him and nourished him with her milk.
    The activity of this beast did not pass unnoticed and one
day the herdsmen followed it and came upon Bou Ghanem
while he was feeding. He was seized and brought before the
prince, who ordered him burned alive. A wood pile was
quickly built and the flames had already begun licking at Bou
Ghanem when he suddenly freed himself from the pole to
which he was bound, seized Yaqub's son, placed him on the
fire in his stead, and, transformed into a crow, fled.
    This miraculous event occasioned endless commentary,

but on the next day, on the site of the fire, Bou Ghanem appeared, feeding dates to Yaqub's son, whom he held on his knee. Again brought before the prince, he returned his son to him and Yaqub expressed his sorrow for having mistreated Bou Ghanem. As a sign of his repentance, the prince made arrangements for Bou Ghanem to settle nearby, making a gift of all the territory of Foussana and Kasserine to him and his descendants.

Bou Ghanem lived peacefully on the land which had been given him, and which the Fraichich did not yet occupy. He took four wives and each bore him a son. These children were named Djelail, al-Hadj, Daharaoui, and Tliti, and they were the bases of the four major divisions of the tribe which today bear their names."

(Archives of the (French) Ministry of War (Vincennes). Tunisia, carton 29.)

DOCUMENT 9:

"Each Tribe Can Be Seen as a Nation . . . . "

Each tribe can be seen as a nation and, like those of the American savages, each has a chief. He is called a shaikh, which means an old man. He is normally chosen among the elders of the tribe, since the person most distinguished for his maturity of judgment and virtue is the one whom the Arabs deem most worthy of leading them . . . .

Properly speaking, government is neither elective nor hereditary. There are some families which have governed for centuries, but they owe this to their paternalistic administration and to the pleasure all men take in obeying those who try to make them happy. Sons generally succeed their fathers, although this method of acquiring power is not guaranteed by any definitive law, since only election by and approbation of the people allow an individual to take the reins of government . . . .

If the shaikh mistreats his people or is unfaithful to the principles of government, no plot is hatched against him personally, nor does anyone plan a revolution. The whole tribe peacefully abandons the shaikh, who leaves to join another tribe whose chief receives this new member with open arms . . . .

In important matters, the shaikh makes a point of consulting with the head of each tent or family and shows the greatest deference for their opinion.

(Filippo Pananti, *Aventure e osservazioni di Filippo Pananti sopra le coste di Barberia*. Milan, 2nd. edition, 3 vols., 1817, pp. 281ff.)

DOCUMENT 10:

A Collective Granary (An Extract of Practices
Recorded in the 17th Century
and Still in Force in the 20th)

12. Whoever closes the gates of the fortress in a rebellious or unjust spirit and, in so doing, separates the anfaliz from the others, will pay 200 dinars; additionally, he will compensate the owner of the room for anything stolen or damaged as a result.

13. Whoever abandons the fortress with his property in a period of insecurity will pay 50 dinars.

14. Whoever accuses another of theft but cannot prove his charge will pay three pieces of gold.

15. Whoever does not put a door on his storeroom, or removes one which has been there, will pay five pieces of gold.

16. Whoever has been told by the masters of the fortress about matters of shares or bonds in the fortress, either by letter or messenger, and who opposes their requests and does not conform with them within one week, will pay a fine of 10 dirhams for each day he has delayed in addition to whatever the masters of the fortress imposed on him.

17. Whoever erects within the fortress a poorly constructed building or one of inferior wood, will have it torn down. He will pay a fine of two dirhams. The relatives and family of each builder also share responsibility.

(Robert Montagne, "Un magasin collectif de L'Anti-Atlas — L'Agadir des Ikouna," *Hespéris*, 1929, pp. 145-266.)

DOCUMENT 11:

Evaluation and Division of a Prize
Taken by Algerian Corsairs

The frigate of al-Hajj Yaqub, the polacre of Ahmad Rais, the batache (corvette) of Kara Danguezli, the corvette of Rais Hamidu, and the shabbak of Rais Mustafa, captured eight Greek vessels loaded with wheat, paper, soap, and brandy. There follows the appropriation of the spoils. 4 Rajab 1213 (December 12, 1798).

Bandjak[1]	57,865	6 rials
Eight prize crews	603	3
Unloading	1,000	
Diwan	84	
Ourdian[2]	27	
Frigate	43	
	59,623	1 rials

Money Changers	1,620	rials
Bandjak Agent	288	
Jewish Agent[3]	144	
Lookouts	18	
Shops	21	
Weigher	150	
	61,864	1 rials
Port Tax[4]	4,000	rials
	65,864	1 rials
Net Profit	397,062	rials
Half of Net Profit	198,531	
Number of Shares:	3,879	
Amount of Each Share:	51	rials

(The gross profit is 520,791 francs, 75 centimes).
1. The state's share of the gross profit.
2. Agent charged with the surveillance of the port.
3. These two agents oversee the settlement of the prizes.
4. Fixed at 1 percent, paid to the Treasury.

(A. Devoulx, "Le Registre des prises maritimes," *Revue Africaine,* 1871, p.448.)

DOCUMENT 12

Lord Exmouth's Show of Force

The places whence provisions are usually drawn, in time of war, are the Black Sea, the Archipelago, Egypt, and the Barbary States. The first three resources failed us more than once in the course of the late long and arduous struggle, and must always be liable to interruption from war or the plague; but the States of Barbary failed us only when they were themselves suffering under the calamity of famine. Rarely has any of them shown an unwillingness to afford us supplies of cattle and corn, or to furnish our ships of war with fresh provisions, free of all duties, whenever they called at any of these ports; even when at war with Turkey, to which the three states bordering on the Mediterranean are, nominally at least, Pashalicks, they never once attempted to shut their ports against us. In vain did Buonaparte dispatch his emissaries, distribute his bribes, employ his promises and threats, to induce those states to enter into his views, and to withhold those supplies, which, he well knew, would have been the first step towards crippling our fleet, and transferring to France the naval superiority in the Mediterranean. As far, then, as nationalist interests are concerned, it would be an act of madness if Great Britain joined in the Holy League which Sir Sidney Smith and his foreign friends have been projecting. It would be worse than madness. It would be nothing short of a direct infringement of justice and good faith . . . . If, at any time, any of those (treaty) stipulations have been violated by the unruly and piratical subjects of those states, immediate reparation has always been made. The British consuls residing at their ports have invariably been respected above those of any other power; though we have heard, indeed, that one of our consuls at Tangier once wrote to the British admiral commanding at Gibraltar, requesting that a longer flag staff might be sent to him to erect before his door, and stating that the consular influence in the dominions of Morocco depended chiefly on the length of his pole.

"The Barbary States", in the *Quarterly Review,* April, 1816, pp. 142-43.)

DOCUMENT 13

TABLES OF NORTH AFRICAN COMMERCE

TABLE 1
Ships Loaded in Tunisia Entering Marseille

Year	Total Number	Number of Tunisian Vessels
1795-1799	64	14
1800-1804	185	54
1805-1809	77	18
1810-1814	37	7
1815	22	3
	385	96

TABLE 2
Ships Entering the Port of Livorno

Origin	1794-1798	1816-1820	1821-1825	1826-1830
Merchant Ships:				
Algeria	54	69	91	133
Morocco	17	15	6	11
Tripoli	12	57	79	96
Tunisia	228	130	97	133
Total	311	271	273	373
Fishing Boats (Algeria, Tunisia)	—	490	812	490
GRAND TOTALS	311	761	1085	863
Total traffic from the entire Mediterranean	1125	5313	3600	2973

TABLE 3
Venetian Carriers in the Latter Years
of the Most Serene Republic

Year	Departures Registered in Tunis Total	For the Levant
1792	6	5
1793	30	6
1794	59	11
1795	108	0
1796	71	7
1797	10	0
	284	29

TABLE 4
Vessels Leaving Tunisian Ports
Bound for Europe and the Levant

Year	Europe and the Levant	The Levant
1820	105	28
1821	139	33
1822	182	23
1824	151	23
1826	178	19
	755	126

DOCUMENT 14

The Cargo Manifest of a Smyrna-Bound Vessel

(N.B.: Notations about the packages and information pertaining to weight which did not affect the rates have been omitted.)

Tunis, July 9, 1794.

A list of cargo, drawn up in this city for the Venetian brigantine *Il Bravo Montenegrino*, commanded by Captain Lipovaz, for transport and consignment to Smyrna follows:

The shipments of:

Selemo Smila, a Tunisian subject, at his own expense, to Raffl. di Hajm Levi and Sons:

1 crate of caps (chechias) dyed red by cochineal, from his factory.

Isac Selama, a Tunisian subject, at his own expense, to Jf. Haj di Saln. Enriches:

1 crate of the above mentioned caps.

Abm Enriches, a Tunisian subject, at his own expense, to Jf. Haj di Saln. Enriches:

2 crates of the above mentioned caps.

Dd. di Sn. Enriches, etc., Tunisian subjects, at their expense, to Jf. Haj di Sn. Enriches:

3 crates of the above mentioned caps.

Dd. di Abm. Enriches, a Tunisian subject, at his expense, to Raffl. di Hajm Levi and Sons:

2 crates of caps containing 290 dozen, more large than small.

Selemo Azulaj, an Algerian subject, at his expense, to Raffl. di Hajm Levi and Sons:

2 crates of the above mentioned caps.

Lojzada Salamon, etc., Tunisian subjects, at their expense, to Raffl. di Hajm Levi and Sons:

5 casks of sugar — 4,607 rotls

2 bales of pepper — 778 ¼ rotls

1 cask of cochineal in 2 sacks — 115 ½ rotls

Rakmin and Moisé Taib, Tunisian subjects, at their expense, to Raffl. di Hajm Levi and Sons:

1 crate containing 32 dozen red caps.

Abmo. di Sassi Taib, a Tunisian subject, at his own expense, to Raffl. di Hajm Levi and Sons:

1 crate of the above mentioned caps.

Dr. Lagomarini, a neutral subject, and physician of the reigning pasha, at the expense of the recipient, to Raffl. di Hajm Levi and Sons, an Ottoman subject:

2 crates of the above mentioned caps.

The same Dr. Lagomarini, to Isac Haj Enriches, a Tunisian subject:

1 crate of caps.

The above mentioned Dr. Lagomarini, at the expense of the recipient, to Matteo (illegible), a Venetian subject:

11 packets of sugar.

Dd. d'Abm. Enriches, a Tunisian subject, at his expense, to Raffl. di Hajm Levi and Sons:

1 crate of caps containing 161$^{1}/_{6}$ dozen, large and small.

Mojsé Haj di Saln. Darmon, a Tunisian subject, at his expense, to Raffl. di Hajm Levi and Sons:

3 crates of the above mentioned caps.

Abm. Lz. Pignero, a Tunisian subject, at his expense, to Ic. Haj Enriches, etc.:

1 crate of the above mentioned caps.

Biniamin de Abm. Lojzada, a Tunisian subject, at his expense, to Raffl. di Hajm Levi and Sons:

1 crate of stambol.

Gabriel di Saln. Enriches, a Tunisian subject, at his expense, to Ic. Haj di Saml. Lumbroso:

2 crates of caps of various fabrics.

Abm. Haj di Jb. Enriches, a Tunisian subject, to Ic. Haj di Sam l. Lumbroso, a Tunisian subject:

2 crates of caps, large and small.

Salamon Va. Bembaron, a Tunisian subject, at his expense, to Ic. Haj Enriches:

1 crate of the above mentioned caps.

Judia Moati, an Algerian subject, at his expense, to Ic. Haj Enriches:

1 purse containing 85 Venetian sequins and 50 Spanish piasters.

The same, at the expense and risk of If. Zeyari, of Algiers, to Raffl. di Hajm Levi and Sons:

1 purse containing 305 Spanish pieces of gold.

If. Franchetti, etc., Tunisian subjects, at their expense, to Franchetti and Co.:

5 crates of red caps.

The above mentioned Franchettis, at their expense, to Franchetti, etc.:

1 crate of caps.

The above named Franchetti, at his expense, to Jf. Haj di Saml. Lumbroso:

1 crate of caps.

Abm. di Dd. Tapia, etc., Tunisian subjects, to Raffl. di Hajm Levi and Sons:

4 crates containing 546 red caps.

Boccara, Tapia, etc., Tunisian subjects, at their expense, to Raffl. di Hajm Levi and Sons:

1 crate containing 104 dozen caps.

Dd. di Saln. Enriches, a Tunisian subject, at his expense, to Isac Haj Enriches, etc.:

1 crate of caps.

Approximately 74 cases of the above mentioned caps loaded by various Moorish merchants, Tunisian subjects, without manifest.

Signed in the original,
Captain P. Lipovaz

(State Archives of Venice. 5 Savi alla Mercanzia, B 769.)

DOCUMENT 15

*The Proclamation of Moulay Slimane
By the People of Fez*

This is the text of the *bai'a* (oath of allegiance) of the people of Fez:

Praised be the One God!

May God pray for our Lord Muhammad, his family, and his companions!

Praise unto God who has created through the caliphate unity between religious and worldly matters; who has bestowed upon the caliph the highest rank; who has caused the sun to shine on the world; who has lit the paths of the earth; who, thanks to the caliph, ordains the form of earthly life and life in the hereafter; who has established through the caliph the unification of the hearts of his servants, whether city or country people; who has appointed the caliph as the protector of life, property, and honor; who, through the caliph, binds the arms of oppressors and prevents them from succeeding in their corrupt undertakings; who, through the caliph, watches over men's affairs and the execution of the sacred laws, pleas, and judgments; who has raised a torch to guide men along the prescribed path and to summon them to truth, so that in his encompassing shadow the strong and the weak, the evil and the noble are sheltered. Blessed be He who has decreed the good path and led the way along it; who has not abandoned man to his own devices but instead has given him orders and prohibitions, has put him on guard against his passions, and has furnished him with the means to fulfill his obligatory and superogatory duties. He is the fairest of judges! If God had not provided for man's mutual support, the universe would surely have become the prey of corruption. But God is filled with benevolence for the world. One of the marks of His mercy is the creation of kings and the building of roads, for if He permitted anarchy, men would devour each other and the world would be ruined. Without the Caliphate there would be no security on the roads and the strong would rob the weak.

May prayers and salvation attend him who has been sent out of compassion for God's creatures, who is the source and root of all that exists, complete perfection, the lord of the friends of God, the imam of the prophets, and the leader of all pure people; may they attend his family which has the right to universal glory of the highest magnitude; may they attend his companions, the orthodox caliphs, guides along the proper path who established the bases of the religion, fixed its rules and taught that the Prophet (God bless him and grant him salvation) said: "God has bestowed the privilege of ruling on the tribe of Quraish and has sent down the revelation: God gives power to whomever He pleases."

God (glory to Him, He alone endures and is eternal) decided that death should be inevitable and reach even he who was burdened with immense powers, carrying him to the place where He pardons, thereby compelling the population to choose an imam (May God place him in paradise and shower on his tomb waves of mercy and pardon!), recalling these words of the Prophet (May prayers and salvation fall upon him): "He who dies without a *bai'a* suspended on his neck dies a pagan death." Anxious to know who to call to these important duties and who would approach them in the proper spirit, the people devoted their thoughts and imagination to meditation. Good direction and divine protection have shown them someone who has grown in piety, virtue, self-respect, devotion, the assiduous study of religion, the zealous search for the ornaments of laudable works, someone who has drawn attention to himself by his intelligence, his alert spirit, cleverness, purity, nobility of character, spirit of determination, political ability, knowledge of affairs, and experience. This is a young man in whom God has united strength with gentleness, whom He has clothed with consideration and respect, and whose power and glory He has increased. He is an intrepid hero, a courageous chief of pure and spotless qualities, of glorious and obvious works, of high rank, standing alone in his time. Abourrabi Moulana Slimane, son of the Prince of the Faithful Moulana Muhammad, son of the Prince of the Faithful Moulana Abdullah, son of the Prince of the Faithful Moulana Isma'il, son of Moulana Echcherif. The people of this Idrisid capital and the lands surrounding it have agreed to take him as chief and imam; they view his elevation to the Emirate and Caliphate as a good omen and are eager to designate him and give him their *bai'a*, contracted under the banners of victory, and whose happiness grows in the realms of peace. All the important notables joins in this *bai'a*, as do the leading people of the age, the masters of the country's fate, and those who accept or reject the law, including the ulama and savants, the muftis and magistrates, respected and generous sharifs, warriors, government officials, military leaders, city dwellers and Arabs who hold the highest rank in every matter, and the 'Abid and Berber armies. The *bai'a* has been reached, God be praised, on the basis of piety, and should reinforce and reaffirm the strength of Islam. It is a perfect *bai'a*, fulfilling all the necessary conditions, in conformity with the traditional rules of the community, and free from violence, trouble, or pressure. Everyone agrees to it and accepts it, promising to respect its holder by their submission and obedience. Witnesses have freely given evidence against themselves and in that respect have filled the sacred prescriptions of God.

May God allow this *bai'a* to be a source of mercy for His creatures, and bring about the reign of justice and truth! May He strengthen by His aid, His power, His protection, and His direction he who accepts it. Through him may God revive the Tradition of our Lord and Master Muhammad (May God pray for him, grant him salvation, ennoble him and sanctify him):

"Happy is the country which has placed its destiny in the hands of one who will protect it, spare its blood, overcome its enemies, repel its aggressors, support the holy law, and restore its foundations, announcing the truth and clarifying its meaning!" May God help him and help others through him! May He help him triumph over heresy and error and disperse oppression and corruption, and may He leave the caliphate in his family until the Last Judgment.

May God pray for our Lord Muhammad, the Seal of the Prophets, for his family and all his companions, for those who report their words and receive their teachings. Amen.

The 18th of the sacred month of Rajab in the year 1206 of the Hijra of the Elect (May he have the best prayers and the purest salvation).

The poorest of the servants of the Most High, the servant of God, Muhammad Ettaoudi ben Ettaleb Ben Souda Elmourri (May God protect and encompass him). The names of the witnesses follow.

(*Kitab elistiqsa li-akhbaridoual elmagrib elaqsa,* in *Archives marocaines,* vol. 9, 1906.)

DOCUMENT 16

The Pacification of Morocco Under Moulay Slimane

1. In the name of the Almighty and Merciful God — there is none so great as He.

To my servant, El-Medy Seydi Alcalde and all my soldiers.

You know the Province where we have been. God has allowed me to capture most of its inhabitants; I have decapitated 1,600 people, exclusive of those, whose number is unknown, killed by my troops.

There are a great many prisoners.

All the houses have been destroyed, while their horses, mules, and cattle, along with all their grains have fallen into the hands of my troops.

All the trees have been cut down, and the few people who have escaped have fled into the mountains. Not a single one of my troops has died.

I salute you.

Written the 14th of Kaada, 1231.

(Translation of a letter from the sovereign to his governors, October 4, 1816.)

2. The king ordered the punishment of the governor general and the fourteen lieutenant governors of Aytata Province to be executed as follows:

4 to be sawed between two boards.
4 to have their hands and feet cut off.
4 to lose one foot and one hand only.
3 to be decapitated.

(Extract from a letter of October 11, 1816, sent by the Governor of Tangiers to all the Consuls. French Ministry of Foreign Affairs Archives. Morocco, *Consular Correspondence*, vol. 24.)

DOCUMENT 17

The Capture of Algiers, As Seen by an Algerian

In short, I ask myself why my country should be shaken to its foundations and all the roots of its vitality attacked? Moreover, in examining the situation of other states around us, none seem condemned to suffer consequences quite like those fated for us. I see Greece aided and then firmly established as a state after tearing itself away from the Ottoman Empire. I see the Belgian people separated from Holland because of their different political and religious principles. I see free people everywhere showing concern over the Poles and the reestablishment of their nationality, and I even see the English government make its glory immortal by the emancipation of Negroes, while the British Parliament spends a half-million pounds to promote that emancipation, but when I think again of the country of Algiers, I see its unfortunate inhabitants placed in the yoke of arbitrary government, of extermination, and of all the plagues of war. And all these horrors are committed in the name of a free France.

(Hamdan ben Othmane Khoja, *Aperçu historique et statistique sur la régence d'Alger intitulé en Arabe Le Miroir,* Paris, 1833, pp. i-ii.)

. . . . And by the Moroccans

Tangiers, July 13. 4 PM. The capture of Algiers, announced by courrier, has thrown all the Moors into consternation.

(French Foreign Affairs Ministry Archives. Morocco, *Political Correspondence,* vol.3.)

The Capture of Algiers as Seen from Marseille

Statement of the Municipal Council to the King (July 26, 1830). In addition to the content of the message, its style should also be considered, particularly since popular rioting which would force King Charles X from the French throne would break out in Paris on July 28. The king, in all probability, never saw these protestations of support from Marseille for his policies.

Sire: Your beautiful city of Marseille, more than any other part of your realm, should experience the consequences of the memorable success which your forces have just achieved. Earlier, as the troops readied themselves in this city it had, amid acclamations of love, offered its thanks to the noble son of France who had, by his presence, given life to these glorious preparations for victory. Accompanying this great expedition with all its good wishes, the city followed the rapid and exciting operations with a solicitude which in no way lessens its confidence in the plans ordered in your wisdom. Filled with joy now that the goal has been realized, the city values all the more the blessing, just as it loves all the more the hand from which it has received it.

(Municipal Archives of Marseille, I D 51, page 156. Cited by P. Guiral, *Marseille et l'Algérie*, p. 50.)

L'Echo Provençal, April 17, 1830
    Who knows what changes we are destined to bring about in these famous, but desolate regions, debased for centuries by the tyranny of Muhammad's followers? Who knows if, in a few years, under the protection of our kings, arts and sciences and commerce will not flourish where today barbarity and ignorance rule and where the banner of the false prophet will soon undoubtedly bow before the flag of France and the revered symbol of Christianity.

L'Echo Provençal, July 21, 1830
    Algiers has just surrendered to our soldiers.
    The cross has been raised where the crescent once shone.

(Cited in P. Guiral, *op. cit.,* pp. 50-51.)

Letter from Charles Fortuné, Bishop of Marseille, to the Chief Chaplain of France:
    Monseigneur,
        The happy news of the capture of Algiers has stimulated the liveliest desire in the hearts of all missionaries to go and water with their sweat this wasteland; they insistently ask me to request of Your Eminence the favor that they be included among the laborers who will preach the faith in the conquered lands . . . .

(Cited by P. Guiral, *op. cit.,* p. 51.)

International Reactions: In England

But now, Algiers being taken, what is to be done with it?
. . . the improvement of Algiers would unquestionably tend to increase our commerce: the wants of a barbarous race would be multiplied, and the desire of European inventions communicated to their neighbors. The nations of Africa to the north of the Great Desert must of necessity turn their attention to agriculture instead of piracy, and we should be able to import from thence many commodities which we are now obliged to seek from beyond the Atlantic. It is an illiberal policy, as we think, to prevent the civilization of a barbarous people and to insist upon their being cast back into their previous state of grossness, lest the new possessors of their country should experience an increase of power. Besides, France upbraids us with the misgovernment and oppression of India: we should be curious to know how she would govern Algeria.

(Extract from *The Times*, July 14, 1830.)

International Reactions: In Switzerland

A desirable success has just crowned a glorious expedition directed against the most powerful of the African states which was a haven for brigands. It promises security in the Mediterranean, will cut the irons prepared for Christian slaves, and will again restore peace and civilization to those shores made famous in antiquity which, after centuries of a long eclipsed splendor, were the frightful arena of the wildest customs.

(The President of the Swiss Diète, Berne, July 6, 1830. Cited by *Le Moniteur universel*, July 18, 1830.)

Appendix 2

Appendix 2

PROBLEMS OF INTERPRETATION

The Algiers Affair

The conquest was initially interpreted as a legitimate reprisal for an insult against France. (See especially the early years of *Revue Africaine* or, more clearly, H.-D. de Grammont's *Histoire d'Alger sous la domination turque (1515-1838)* (Paris, 1887). More accurate descriptions of the matter appear in Gabriel Esquer, *La Prise d'Alger* (Paris, 1929), and Charles-André Julien *(Histoire de l'Algérie contemporaine).* The latter condenses the issue in one sentence:

"Shady business deals engineered by the powerful Jewish merchants of Algiers with the complicity of disreputable politicians in Paris; an incident provoked by a questionable diplomat; an expedition led by a discredited general; a victory received with indifference or hostility by the public and followed by the collapse of the dynasty which proclaimed its value — these were the peculiar beginnings of the

French conquest of Algeria."

The characters in the drama included the Jewish merchants Bacri and Busnach who had shipped wheat to France between 1793 and 1798 and remained French creditors. Their accomplice was Talleyrand, whom they involved in their business and from whom they obtained recognition of greatly inflated claims. With Deval, the consul general named by Talleyrand in 1815, discredited in Algiers, they tricked Hussain Dey, whose claims were ignored. Pushed to the limit, the dey struck the consul with his fly-whisk with well-known results.

The Capture of Algiers
As a Victory Over the "Pirates"

Privateering and the condition of Christian slaves fostered a genre of literature which historiography adopted in its account. From this perspective, the capture of Algiers was a victory of civilization over barbarism, since it finally purged the Mediterranean of pirates. For example, Gabriel Esquer wrote in his work already cited (page 15):

"Contacts between the Regency and the Christian states had been characterized by the humiliation of the civilized nations by a pirate chief."

As late as 1964, Salvatore Bono *(I corsari barbareschi)* subscribed to this interpretation. Several historians have, however, clarified the role of the Christians, which was not only that of victim. (See the references to studies by Emerit, Mathiex, Fisher, and Godechot in the section of the bibliography concerning privateering). After measuring the significance of privateering in Tunisia (Christian slaves and black slaves in Tunis in the 18th century), this work has attempted to assess its impact — in the final analysis a rather limited one — in the wider Maghribi economy.

Fernand Braudel has concluded this debate with these

words *(The Mediterranean and the Mediterranean World in the Age of Philip II,* Vol. II): "The activity of pirates in the Mediterranean as a whole has been greatly over-estimated. Too much attention has been paid to the protests and arguments of the inhabitants of Christian shores. . . ."

States, Nations, and National Feeling

In a brilliant but irritatingly ethnocentric book, E. F. Gautier wrote:

"One great problem continually dominates all North African history, reappearing on every page. While the central theme of our European national histories remains the same — the successive stages by which the State, then the nation, developed — the central theme in the Maghrib is the sequence of specific failures which led to total failure." *(L'Islamisation de l'Afrique du Nord, les siècles obscurs du Maghrib,* Paris, 1927).

Happily, European historiography has freed itself from this problematical issue, and the constitution of states is no longer its major preoccupation. Moreover, the conviction that the destiny of Europe, and of France in particular, was exemplary, has ended. Nevertheless, several authors have followed Gautier's lead and have sought explanations for the inability of a nation or a state to develop. Among them are Charles-André Julien *(Histoire de l'Afrique du Nord),* H. Isnard, J. Despois, and G. H. Bousquet. The interpretations they have advanced will be examined below.

On the other hand, recent liberation movements have given added meaning to the debate on the existence of nations before colonization. Yves Lacoste, André Nouschi, and André Prenant have attempted to prove that a national collectivity was emerging on the eve of the conquest *(L'Algérie, passé et présent).* Separating the problem of the state from that of the nation, Xavier Yacono has rehabilitated the Turkish state by demonstrating that the Turkish era was not a period of permanent anarchy and that Algeria was "more than a sterile, depopulated region." *(La Colonisation des plaines du Chélif)*. Finally, Mustafa Lacheraf *(L'Algérie, nation et société)* has emphasized the strength of the resistance and the cohesion of the rural people. Along the same lines, Germain Ayache has examined the national consciousness in Morocco in the 19th century. The two pillars of the Moroccan nation were the rural tribes and the sovereign. Unlike them, the bourgeoisie of the ports managed to endure foreign intrusion without difficulty. ("Le Sentiment national dans le Maroc du XIXe siècle," *Revue Historique*, vol. 240, Oct.-Dec., 1968. pp. 393-410). In the Tunisian case, Charles-André Julien has reservations about the use of the concept of national sentiment, suggesting a distinction of different levels:

"Do popular demonstrations necessarily reveal the appearance of national feeling? The decision must be nuanced. I believe that patriotism and national feeling are too often confused. Patriotism, bursting forth from the soil, is simultaneously simple and powerful, obeying instinct rather than reason. It is quite different with national sentiment, which is necessarily more complex and based on a collective need." (Foreward to B. Slama, *L'Insurrection de 1864 en Tunisie*, Tunis, 1967, p. ix).

The Paralysis of the Maghrib

Interpretations of the weakness of the idea of states in North Africa and the economic and technical retardation of the area are often interrelated. Consequently, they are considered together here.

The geographic theory — a semiarid climate, the absence of a center of convergence, the limited prolongation of the plains — was first advocated by E.-F. Gautier *(op. cit.)* and later expounded by Jean Despois *(L'Afrique du Nord,* 1949) and H. Isnard ("Le Sol, l'homme, ou l'histoire? Sur les destins de l'Afrique du Nord," *Annales, ESC,* 1950, pp. 120-24). One objection to this thesis is that these difficulties occur only when the technical skills at man's disposal are weakly developed. In addition, this reasoning cannot be chronologically generalized, because the medieval Maghrib had brilliant phases of progress. Finally, the geographic factors lend themselves to contradictory interpretations. For example, did not Morocco, with both Atlantic and Mediterranean coasts, close to Europe, and in contact with sub-Saharan African, have a natural vocation for foreign commerce? Should not it have been more open to European influences than other areas? Yet it has been shown that this was not at all the case.

A second theory rests on Berber inertia. The second edition of Charles-André Julien's *History of North Africa,* edited and revised by Roger LeTourneau, closes with these remarks:

"Different though the development of the two Regencies was, the Turks nevertheless failed to impart any fresh impetus to the age-old Maghrib. In the one as in the other, Berber inertia won the day, so that at the beginning of the 19th century the entire Maghrib was living, withdrawn into its shell, in accordance with standards that had held for thousands of years, and without having been able to evolve in the direction of statehood in its modern form."

More frankly, Georges-Henri Bousquet *(Les Berbères,* 1957) denounced "the congenital impotence of the Berbers to create anything."

These assertions provoke two observations: (1) Since Tunisia was almost totally Arabized (98 percent of the population), this theory cannot apply to it. (2) There is no Berber race Berber unity is linguistic, even though the language is subdivided into a great number of local dialects, and in no way ethnic. In addition, the ethnic theory would be rejected today for obvious reasons.

Along with the indomitable Berbers, some have blamed the nomads, and especially the Hilalian Invasion of the 11th century, for North Africa's troubles. Once again, E.-F. Gautier pioneered the way. Much more recently, a lively controversy opposed Roger Idris, a follower of Gautier, to Jean Poncet in the review *Annales* (1967, No. 5, pp. 1099-1120; 1968, No. 2, pp. 390-96; and no. 3, pp. 660-62). Jean Poncet stressed the crisis in the Kairouan state before the arrival of the Hilalians, thereby minimizing their destructive role. Xavier Yacono *(op. cit.)* defends a similar view. While awaiting new investigations — especially archaeological ones — to rejuvenate the older texts, it seems reasonable to agree with Jacques Berque that "these noble parasites have been very much maligned . . . . However, they would not have succeeded in spreading their life style as far as they did if they had not found some natural base for it and some correlation with the economy of the Berber herders." ("La Connaissance au temps'd'Ibn Khaldoun," *Contributions à la sociologie de la connaissance,* vol.1, 1967, pp. 35-70).

Jean Despois has singled out another guilty party, the mountaineer. ("Géographie et histoire en Afrique du Nord, retouches à une thèse," *Eventail de l'histoire vivante, mélanges à Lucien Febvre,* Paris, 1953, vol.1, pp. 187-94). The mountains offer a setting for dissidence, are the refuge of a frozen civilization, and play only a negative role. This interpretation, of limited utility for Algeria and Morocco, is meaningless for Tunisia.

Another hypothesis provokes the same objection, this time because it is inapplicable to Morocco: the role of the foreigner, or colonialism. Algeria and Tunisia were only rarely free from foreign rulers, who succeeded one another from the Carthaginians to the Turks. (See Isnard's article cited above). Xavier de Planhol has returned to mòst of these stereotypes in *Les Fondements géographiques de l'histoire de l'Islam,* Paris, 1968.

The Role of Islam

Since none of this information furnishes a general explanation, some scholars have looked to Islam. This hypothesis, if it could be supported, would apply not only to the Maghrib, but would also explain the economic retardation of the entire Muslim world. Christian contemporaries had already thought about this. The argument is still defended, particularly by J. Austruy (*L'Islam face au développement économique*, Paris, 1961). A colloquium held in Paris in 1960 reached different conclusions ("L'Evolution économique, sociale, et culturelle des pays d'Islam s'est-elle montrée défavorable à la formation d'un capitalisme de type occidental?" Unpublished). In *Islam and Capitalism*, Maxime Rodinson has approached the issue and succeeded in demonstrating that Islam's prescriptions posed no obstacle to either the development of modern economic forms or the birth of a capitalist mentality. The Muslim world has utilized certain forms of capitalism, but these have never constituted the dominant sector of the economy.

In the same sense, Pierre Bourdieu (*The Algerians*) notes that "the fundamental traits of the traditionalist spirit found in Algerians — submission to nature and to time — can be observed in most societies unfamiliar with industrial civilization and thus cannot be described as consequences of adhesion to Islam."

However, since the capitalist economy did not develop *sua sponte*, the question arises as to why the North Africans did not borrow the techniques of the Christians. H. Isnard tries to answer this question by observing that, since the 15th century, North Africa remained a battlefield of Islam against Christianity — a position which rendered dialogue impossible ("Le sol, l'homme ou l'histoire? Sur les destins de l'Afrique du Nord," *Annales, ESC,* 1960, pp. 120-24.)

The Mode of Production

Finally, some writers have analyzed North Africa's socio-economic background to find explanations for its lack of dynamism. This entailed defining the means of production as well as the links between production and social stratification.

Several authors have concluded that feudalism characterized this society. In Morocco, a prime example was the Seksawa tribe which Jacques Berque studied *(Les Seksawa)*, because it included great lordly domains and, even more importantly, was marked by strong links of personal dependence. The history of Morocco, as Brignon, Amine, and others present it *(Histoire du Maroc)*, takes the form of a permanent conflict between forces of cohesion and forces of disintegration, with the great feudal chiefs, periodically strengthening their positions at the expense of the Makhzan, cast in the latter role.

At the other end of the Maghrib, Jean Poncet *(La Colonisation et l'agriculture européennes en Tunisie depuis 1881)* believes that a process of feudalization — a splitting of political power and the creation of great landed estates — can be observed on the eve of the establishment of the protectorate. In Algeria, Yves Lacoste, André Nouschi, and André Prenant on the one hand, and Mustafa Lacheraf on the other, all view feudalism as a deterrent to economic development and the emergence of a national collectivity. In a more systematic fashion, René Gallissot ("Precolonial Algeria," in *Economy and Society*, vol. 4, 1975) has devoted himself to establishing the impact of feudal rulers and lords expropriating peasant labor.

The publication of such Marxist works as *Pre-Capitalist Economic Formations,* with an introduction by Eric Hobsbawm (London, 1964) and *Fondements de la critique de l'économie politique* (Paris, 1967) have reinvigorated this debate. In addition to the western European model of evolution (passage from a slave-holding society to feudalism and to capitalism), Marx described other social models, including ancient society, the Teutonic type, the Asiatic mode of production, and others, which had in common the absence of antagonistic classes and a relative inertia.

The dominant socioeconomic framework of the precolonial Maghrib could readily be construed as, in effect, a variation on the archaic model. As early as 1930, Robert Montagne, studying *Les Berbères et le Makhzen dans le sud du Maroc,* observed two social structures: one with extensive holdings of the feudal type and the other with independent entities which were patriarchal and more democratic. The second type was older, and Montagne was able to date the recent appearance of the other. This restored "the view of a society which, in form, had remained very archaic, and which presents us, even today, with the sight which the oldest civilizations of the Mediterranean offered three millenia ago."

Broadening the field of observation, this work has tried to describe a society which is founded on family unity and which succeeds in satisfying the needs of all members of the group by a democratic division of the land and the means of production, and by a network of linkages and exchanges through which the poor and misfortunate find alleviation of their misery. In this society, inequalities of wealth are indisputable, as is the emergence of areas of control. On the other hand, feudalism appears, at least belatedly.

This structure can, and did, last so long as nothing occurred to modify its operation. If medical progress caused a demographic explosion or if the intrusion of an advanced monetary economy upset the subsistence economy and depreciated its products, the destruction of the equilibrium would be inevitable.

Several studies indicate this. Marcel Emerit ("Au début du XIXe siècle: les tribus privilégiées en Algérie," *Annales,* 1966, no. 1, pp. 44-58) challenges the notion of feudalism as applied to Turkish Algeria, and G. Lazarev does the same for Morocco ("Les Concessions foncières au Maroc," *Annales marocaines de sociologie,* 1968, pp. 99-135). Pierre Bourdieu *(op. cit.)* observed in Algerian society social differences but not class opposition. The analyses collected by Pitt-Rivers *(Mediterranean Countrymen, Essays in the Social Anthropology of the Mediterranean,* Paris and The Hague, 1963) also stress the social organization based on the agnatic family.

This debate has some prolongations. For the present period, some individuals describe the destruction of traditional structures (André Nouschi, *Enquête sur le niveau de vie des populations rurales constantinoises de la conquête jusqu'en 1919),* while others, without denying the crisis of these structures, draw attention to the permanence of the "inviolate" (Jacques Berque and Pierre Bourdieu). It is an essential debate which would benefit from, and which deserves, new research.

Since the French publication of this book, the argument over modes of production has continued (Amin, Benachenhou, Chentouf, and Djeghloul). It is now imperative that a social history of the North African countries be written, rather than continuing a controversy which has become theological. Moreover, it would be useful to bear in mind Pierre Bourdieu's criticisms of "negative explanations of an impoverished materialism." This author insists on "the determinant contributions which ethical and mythical images can bring to the reproduction of the economic order of which they are the product" *(Esquisse d'une théorie de la pratique,* p. 12).

BIBLIOGRAPHY

A few preliminary remarks about the bibliography are necessary. First, the Maghrib of this book excludes Tripolitania because of the risk of confusion in attempting to extend the area examined. The historical analysis of the Regency of Tripoli has scarcely begun. Moreover, to have covered all of North Africa in a single glance would have meant erasing regional contrasts and finding unity only at the price of excessive simplifications. Merely by limiting the aim of this study, the possibility of shading its presentation has, to some degree, already been sacrificed.

Severed from Tripolitania, our Maghrib is also denied an analysis of its natural environment. Without accepting geographical determinism, it remains incontestable that the level of technology in the 18th century allowed natural factors — climate, soil, and vegetation — to play a major role. It is fitting, then, to ascertain information about these basic conditions from geographers, including:

Birot, Pierre, and Dresh, Jean. *La Méditerranée occidentale*. Vol. I. Paris, 1953.

Despois, Jean. *L'Afrique du nord*. 3rd edition. Paris, 1964.

Despois, Jean, and René Raynal. *Géographie de l'Afrique du nord-ouest*. Paris, 1967.

Another observation: much knowledge about North African societies comes from reading fundamental studies which are not always the works of historians properly speaking and which do not necessarily concern the period concentrated on in this book. Among the best of these are:

Berque, Jacques. *Les Seksawa. Recherches sur les structures sociales du Haut Atlas occidental.* Paris, 1954.

Bourdieu, Pierre. *The Algerians.* Boston, 1962.

Braudel, Fernand. *The Mediterranean and the Mediterranean World in the Age of Philip II.* 2 vols. New York, 1972.

Despois, Jean. *La Tunisie orientale. Sahel et basses steppes.* Paris, 1955.

Finally, in North African historiography the fundamental and most important work remains Charles-André Julien's *Histoire de l'Afrique du Nord.* 2nd. edition. 2 vols. Paris, 1951 and 1952. Volume 2, covering the period from the Arab conquest until 1830, as edited and revised by Roger LeTourneau, has been translated into English as *History of North Africa.* London, 1969.

In the bibliography which follows, some recent books and articles which appeared after the publication of the French edition of this work have been included.

RESEARCH AIDS

I. BIBLIOGRAPHICAL COLLECTIONS

Detailed bibliographies appear in the works by Julien and Despois cited above. In addition, see:

Bibliography of the Barbary States.

Henry Spencer Ashbee. *A Bibliography of Tunisia.* Vol. II. London, 1889.

Robert Lambert Playfair. *A Bibliography of Algeria.* Vol. III. London, 1889.

———. *Supplement to the Bibliography of Algeria.* London, 1898.

——— and R. Brown. *Bibliography of Morocco.* Vol. IV. London, 1892.

Bel, Alfred. *La Religion musulmane en Berbérie.* Vol. I. Paris, 1938.

Marçais, Georges. *Manuel d'art musulman.* 2 vols. Paris, 1926.

Ministère de la Guerre. *L'Afrique Française du Nord. Bibliographie militaire des ouvrages français ou traduits en français et des articles des principales revues françaises relatifs à l'Algérie, à la Tunisie et au Maroc de 1830 à 1926.* 4 vols. Paris, 1931.

For Algeria:

Julien, Charles-André. *Histoire de l'Algérie contemporaine, I: La Conquête et les débuts de la colonisation (1827-1871)*. Paris, 1964. This book contains an exhaustive critical bibliography which includes call numbers for the major libraries of Paris and Algiers. The work clearly replaces everything which has preceded it.

For Morocco:

Cenival, Pierre de; Funck-Brentano, Christian; Bousser, Marcel. *Bibliographie marocaine (1923-1933)*. Paris, 1937.

Institut des Hautes Etudes Marocaines. *Initiation au Maroc*. 3rd. edition. Rabat, 1946.

Miège, Jean. *Le Maroc et l'Europe (1830-1894)*. Vol. I. Paris, 1961.

Tables et index des publications de l'Institut des Hautes Etudes Marocaines (1915-1935). Paris, 1936. This collection was continued until 1953 by Jacques Riche and Odette Lille.

Terrasse, Henri. *History of Morocco*. Casablanca, 1952.

For Tunisia:

Bono, Salvatore. "Fonti e documenti italiani per la storia della Tunisia" in *Quaderni dell'Instituto italiano di Cultura di Tunisi*, I, 1969, pp. 1-21.

Brunschvig, Robert; Pignon, J., et al. *Initiation à la Tunisie*. Paris, 1950.

Despois, Jean. *La Tunisie*. Paris, 1961.

Rouard de Card, Edgard. *Bibliographie des ouvrages relatifs à la Berbérie au XVIIe et au XVIIIe siècles*. Paris, 1911. Supplemented, 1917.

II. GENERAL WORKS

Hodgson, Marshall. *The Venture of Islam*. 3 Vols. Chicago, 1974.

Miquel, André. *L'Islam et sa civilisation*. Paris, 1968.

For Algeria, Julien's *Histoire de l'Algérie contemporaine* opens with a description of the Regency before the capture of Algiers, which constitutes an excellent updating of existing information.

Lacoste, Yves; Nouschi, André, and Prenant, André. *L'Algérie, passé et présent. Le cadre et les étapes de la constitu-*

tion de l'Algérie actuelle. Paris, 1960.

To the works already noted on Morocco must be added this very fine collective work:

Brignon, Jean; Amine, Abdelaziz; Boutaleb, Brahim; Martinet, Guy; and Rosenberger, G. *Histoire du Maroc.* Paris and Casablanca, 1967.

For all three countries, the *Encyclopedia of Islam* provides a wealth of information on all subjects.

An overview appears in:

Cherif, Muhammad. "L'Histoire de l'Afrique du nord jusqu'à l'indépendance. Le Maghreb dans l'histoire," *Introduction à l'Afrique du Nord contemporaine.* Paris, 1975. pp. 17-49.

An historiographical critique is:

Laroui, Abdallah. *The History of the Maghreb.* Princeton, 1977.

III. JOURNALS AND COLLECTIONS

Archives Berbères. Vols. I-IV, 1915-1920. Paris.

Archives Marocaines. Vols. I-XXXIV, 1904-1936. Paris.

Cahiers de Tunisie. This periodical is the successor of *Revue Tunisienne.*

Hespéris. 1921-1960. Rabat. Since 1960, *Hespéris-Tamuda.*

IBLA. Journal of the Institut des Belles Lettres Arabes, Tunis (1937-). More concerned with ethnography and literature than with history.

Oriente Moderno. Rome (1921-).

Revue Africaine. This journal, begun in 1856, was the oldest one dealing with the Maghrib. It was published in Algiers for over a hundred years.

Revue de l'Occident musulman et de la Méditerranée. (1966-). Many former contributors to *Revue Africaine* write in this journal.

Revue Tunisienne. Tunis (1894-1948).

La Revue Tunisienne des Sciences sociales. Tunis (1964-). This work is more concerned with geography and sociology than with history.

Villes et Tribus du Maroc. Vols. I-VII, 1915-1921. Vols. VIII-XI, 1930-1932. Paris.

Many basic articles also appear in major French journals including *Annales, Revue Historique,* and *Revue d'Etudes Islamiques.*

Two new periodicals have appeared since the French publication of this book. They are:

Archives Nationales, Algiers.
Revue d'Histoire Maghrébine, Tunis.

IV. ARCHIVES

Published archival material:

Plantet, Eugène. *Correspondance des deys d'Alger avec la cour de France (1579-1833).* 2 vols. Paris, 1889.

_____. *Correspondance des beys de Tunis et des consuls de France avec la cour, 1577-1830.* 3 vols. Paris, 1893-99.

North African archives:

The archives of the Regency of Algiers are now available in Algiers. Certain series are on microfilm at the Archives de la France d'Outre' Mer in Aix-en-Provence, France, and at the Archives Nationales in Paris. The two following articles concern the Moroccan archives:

LeTourneau, Roger. "Les Archives musulmanes en Afrique du Nord." *Archivum,* 4 (1954), pp. 175-78.

Ayache, Germain. "La Question des archives historiques marocaines." *Hespéris-Tamuda,* 1961, pp. 311-26.

For Tunisia, see: :

Mantran, Robert. *Inventaire des documents d'archives turcs du Dar el bey.* Paris, 1961. The most important material, however, is in Arabic, and that is what has been extensively used in this work.

An important recent work is:

Chevallier, D., ed. *Les Arabes par leurs archives, XVIe-XXe siècles.* Paris, 1975.

Archives of the Ports:

These furnish information about commercial contacts between the Maghrib and Europe as well as reporting on health conditions in various ports of the Mediterranean. The collections utilized were those of Venice, Livorno (Archivio di Stato), and Marseille. The latter, divided between the departmental archives of the Bouches-du-Rhône and the Archives of the Marseille

Chamber of Commerce, are the richest.

Consular Archives:

In France, the National Archives (Fonds Affaires Etrangeres et Marine) preserve consular correspondence until the Revolution. For the later period, one uses the Archives of the Ministry of Foreign Affairs at the Quai d'Orsay. These include consular correspondence, commercial notes, memoirs, and other documents. The Archives of the Ministry of War at Vincennes are less fruitful. Corresponding records may be found in London (Public Record Office), Turin, and Florence (Archivio di Stato).

AFRICA IGNORED

A glimpse of French intellectual output in the 18th century is afforded in the Registres de Privilèges in the Bibliothèque Nationale, Mss. Fr. Nos. 21 960 ff. See also the selection by F. Furet and the afterword by A. Dupront in *Livre et Société dans la France du XVIIIe siècle*. Paris, 1965. Also see:

Estivals, Robert. *La Statistique bibliographique de la France sous la monarchie du XVIIIe siècle*. Paris, 1965.

Dictionaries and Encyclopedias

Bruzen de la Martinière, Antoine. *Grand Dictionnaire géographique, historique, et critique*. Paris, 1768.

Grasset de Saint Sauveur, Jacques. *Tableaux des principaux peuples de l'Europe, de l'Asie, de l'Afrique et de l'Amérique*. Paris, l'an VI.

_____. *Encyclopédie des voyages*. Paris, 1796.

Moreri, Louis. *The Great Historical, Geographical, and Poetical Dictionary*. London, 1694.

Peuchet, Jacques. *Dictionnaire universel de la Géographie commerçante*. Paris, l'an V-l'an VII.

Vosgien. (Jean-Baptiste Ladvocat). *An Historical and Biographical Dictionary*. Cambridge, England, 1799-1801.

Travelogues, Stories about Captivity, and 18th and 19th Century Memoirs:

On the impact of the corsair phenomenon on folklore and literature in the Mediterranean countries, see the brilliant preface of Renzo de Felice to:

Bono, Salvatore. *I Corsari Barbareschi*. Turin, 1964.

On English literature, see the following well documented article:

Lebel, Roland. "Le Maroc dans les relations des voyageurs anglais aux XVIe, XVIIe, et XVIIIe siècles." *Hespéris*, 9 (1929), pp. 269-94.

See also:

Lebel, Roland. *Les Voyageurs français au Maroc. L'Exotisme marocain dans la littérature de voyage*. Paris, 1936.

Vovard, André. *Les Turqueries dans la littérature française, le cycle barbaresque*. Toulouse, 1949.

Ali Bey (Domingo Badia y Leblich). *Travels of Ali Bey in Morocco, Tripoli, Cyprus, Egypt, Arabia, Syria, and Turkey*. 2 vols. Philadelphia, 1816.

Barbier, Charles. *Itinéraire historique et descriptif de l'Algérie*. Paris, 1855.

Caronni, Felice. *Voyage chez les Barbaresques*. Paris, 1805.

Caillé, Jacques. *La Mission du capitaine Burel au Maroc en 1808*. Paris, 1953.

————. "Le Vice-Consul Brousonnet et ses 'mémoires' sur le Maroc." *Hespéris-Tamuda*, 2 (1961), pp. 5-42.

Carette, Antoine-Auguste. "Origine et Migrations des principales tribus de l'Afrique septentrionale et particulièrement de l'Algérie." *Exploration scientifique de l'Algérie pendant les années 1840, 1841, 1842*. Paris, 1853.

Charles-Roux, François. "Un projet de conquête au Maroc présenté par un Français aux ministres de Louis XV en 1748." *Revue de l'histoire des colonies françaises*, 1928, pp. 589-96.

Chenier, Louis. *The Present State of the Empire of Morocco*. London, 1788.

Daumas, Eugène. *Exposé de l'état actuel de la société arabe*. Algiers, 1844.

————. *La Vie arabe et la société musulmane*. Paris, 1869.

———— and Fabar, Paul. *Etudes historiques sur la Grande Kabylie*. Paris, 1847.

Emerit, Marcel. *L'Algérie à l'époque d'Abd el Kader*. Paris, 1951.

————. "Un mémoire inédit de l'Abbé Raynal sur la Tunisie (XVIIIe siècle)." *Revue Tunisienne*, 3-4 (1948), pp. 131-84.

Esquer, Gabriel, ed. *Reconnaissance des villes, forts, et batteries d'Alger (1808).* Toulouse, 1927.

Forteguerri, B. *O più pace, o più guerra. Memoria riguardante il sistema di pace, e di guerra che le potenze europee praticano con le Reggenze di Barberia.* Naples, 1786.

Foucauld, Charles de. *Reconnaissance au Maroc.* Paris, 1888.

Frank, Louis. *Tunis.* Paris, 1862.

Gallico, Augusto. *Tunisi, e i consoli sardi (1816-1834).* Bologna, 1935.

Gråberg di Hemso, Jacob. *Specchio geografico e statistico del impero di Marocco.* Genoa, 1834.

_____. *Cenni statistici e geografici della Reggenza di Algeri.* Milan, 1830.

Grenville Temple, Richard. *Excursions in Algiers and Tunis.* 2 vols. London, 1835.

Höst, Georg. *Nachrichten von Marokos und Fes.* Copenhagen, 1781.

Jackson, G. A. *Algiers. Being a Complete Picture of the Barbary States, Their Government, Law, Religion, and Natural Productions.* London, 1817.

Jackson, James G. *An Account of the Empire of Morocco and the Districts of Sus and Tafilelt.* London, 1809.

Kennedy, Clark. *Algeria and Tunisia in 1845.* 2 vols. London, 1846.

Laugier de Tassy. *A Compleat History of the Piratical States of Barbary.* London, 1750.

Lemprière, William. *A Tour from Gibraltar to Tangier, Sallee, Mogadore, and Santa Cruz.* London, 1791.

MacGill, Thomas. *Account of Tunis.* London, 1811.

Martin, Maria. *History of a Captivity and Sufferings of Mrs. M. Martin, who was Six Years a Captive in Algiers.* Boston, 1807.

Monchicourt, Charles. *Documents historiques sur la Tunisie. Relations inédites de Nyssen, Filippi et Calligaris.* Paris, 1929.

Noah, Mordechai. *Correspondence and Documents Relative to the Attempt to Negotiate for the Release of the American Captives at Algiers.* Washington, 1816.

_____. *Travels in England, France, Spain and the Barbary States, 1813, 1814, and 1815.* New York, 1819.

Mouette, Germain. *The Travels of the Sieur Mouette in the Kingdoms of Fez and Morocco.* London, 1710.

Paddock, Judah. *A Narrative of the Shipwreck of the Ship "Oswego" on the Coast of South Barbary.* New York, 1818.

Pananti, Filippo. *Narrative of a Residence in Algiers.* London, 1830.

Peyssonel, Jean, and Desfontaines, Louis. *Voyages dans les Régences de Tunis et d'Alger.* 2 vols. Paris, 1838.

Pfeiffer, S. *Meine Reise und meine funfjahrige Gefangenshaft in Algier.* Giessen, 1832.

Poiret, Jean-Louis. *Travels Through Barbary in 1785 and 1786.* London, n.d.

Poiron, Jean. *Mémoires concernans l'état présent du Royaume de Tunis.* Paris, 1925.

Puckler-Muskau, Hermann. *Semilasso in Africa. Adventures in Algiers and Other Parts of Africa.* London, 1837.

Raynal, Abbé. *Histoire philosophique et politique des établissements et du commerce des Européens dans l'Afrique septentrionale.* 2 vols. Paris, 1826.

Rehbinder, Johan Adam. *Nachrichten und Bemerkungen über den Algierischen Staat.* 2 vols. Altona, 1798-1800.

Roussier, Paul. "Les Derniers projets et le dernier voyage de Domingo Badia (1815-1818)." *Revue Africaine,* 1930, pp. 36-91.

Rozet, Claude. *Voyage dans la Régence d'Alger.* Paris, 1833.

Saint Gervais, M. de. *Mémoires historiques qui concernent le gouvernement de l'ancien et du nouveau Royaume de Tunis.* Paris, 1736.

Shaler, William. *Sketches of Algiers, Political, Historical, and Civil.* Boston, 1826.

Shaw, Thomas. *Travels and Observations Relating to Several Parts of Barbary and the Levant.* Oxford, 1738.

Stanley, Edward. *Observations on the City of Tunis and the Adjacent Country.* 4 vols. London, 1786.

Venture de Paradis, Jean. *Alger au XVIIIe siècle.* Paris, 1898.

North African Literature

Morocco:

A basic work is:

Levi Provençal, E. *Les Historiens des Chorfa. Essai de littérature historique et bibliographique au Maroc du XVIe au XXe siècles.* Paris, 1922.

al-Nasiri al-Slawi, Ahmad ibn Khalid. *Kitab al-Istiqsa al-akhbar duwal al-Maghrib al-Aqsa.* 4 vols. Cairo, 1894. A French translation appears in *Archives Marocaines* 9 (1906), pp. 1-399 and 10 (1907), pp. 1-424.

al-Zayyani. *al-Tarjama al-mu'arib 'an dwal al-mashriq wa al-maghrib.* A French translation by O. Houdas is entitled *Le Maroc de 1631 à 1812.* Paris, 1886.

Tunisia:

Ibn 'Abd al-Aziz, Hammuda. *Kitab al-Bashi.* vol. I. Tunis, 1970.

Maqdish al-Sfaxi. *Nuzhat al-anzar fi 'aja'ib at-tawarikh wa 'l-akhbar.* Portions are translated by C. A. Nallino in *Venezia e Sfax nel secolo XVIII secondo il cronista arabo Maqdish, Centenario della nascita di Michele Amari,* Vol. I. Palermo, 1910, pp. 306-56.

al-Bagi al-Mas 'udi, Muhammad. *al-Khulasah an-naqiyyah fi umara' Ifriqiyyah.*

Saghir ibn Yusuf, Muhammad. *Mashru' al-milki.* A French translation entitled "Machra el-melki, soixante ans d'histoire de la Tunisie," by V. Serres and Muhammad Lasram, appears in *Revue Tunisienne,* 1895-1900 and in a single volume, *Mechra el Melki, chronique tunisienne, 1705-1771.* Tunis, 1900.

Ibn Abi Diyaf. *Athaf ahl az-zaman.* 7 vols. Tunis, 1963-1965.

Abdesselem, Ahmed. *Les Historiens tunisiens des XVIIe, XVIIIe et XIXe siècles.* Tunis, 1973.

Algeria:

Emerit, Marcel. "L'Etat intellectuel et moral de l'Algérie en 1830." *Revue d'histoire moderne et contemporaine* (July-September, 1954), pp. 201-212.

Dournon, A. "Kitab tarikh Qosantina par el Hadj Ahmed El Mobarek." *Revue Africaine,* no. 289 (1913), pp. 265-306.

DEMOGRAPHIC PROBLEMS

Evaluation of the population and ethnic divisions:

Bennett, Norman. "Christian and Negro Slavery in 18th Century North Africa." *Journal of African History,* I (1960), pp. 65–82.

Bousquet, Georges-Henri. *Les Berbères*. 3rd edition. Paris, 1967.

Boyer, Pierre. "L'Evolution démographique des populations musulmanes du département d'Alger (1830/66-1948)." *Revue Africaine* (1954), pp. 308-53.

Chouraqui, André. *Between East and West: A History of the Jews of North Africa*. Philadelphia, 1968.

Ganiage, Jean. "La Population de la Tunisie vers 1860. Essai d'évaluation d'après les registres fiscaux." *Population*, no. 5 (September-October, 1966), pp. 857-886.

Massignon, Louis. *Le Maroc dans les premières années du XVIe siècle. Tableau géographique d'après Léon l'Africain*. Paris, 1906.

Morsy, Magali. "Moulay Isma'il et l'Armée de métier." *Revue d'histoire moderne et contemporaine* (April-June, 1967), pp. 97-122.

Sebag, Paul. "Les Juifs de Tunisie au XIXe siècle, d'après J.-J. Benjamin II." *Cahiers de Tunisie*, no. 28 (1959), pp. 489-510.

Valensi, Lucette. "Esclaves chrétiens et esclaves noirs à Tunis au XVIIIe siècle." *Annales ESC*, no. 6 (1966), pp. 1267-88.

Yacono, Xavier, "Peut-on évaluer la population de l'Algérie vers 1830?" *Revue Africaine* (1954), pp. 277-307.

Zafrani, Haim. *Les Juifs du Maroc. Vie sociale, économique et religieuse, étude de taqqanot et responsa*. Paris, 1970.

Epidemics and famines

The following works concern epidemics:

Berbrugger, Louis. "Mémoire sur la peste en Algérie." *Exploration Scientifique de l'Algérie*. Paris, 1844.

Gråberg di Hemso, Jacob. *Lettera del Signor Gråberg di Hemso al Signor Luigi Grossi sulla peste di Tangeri negli anni 1818-1819*. Genoa, 1820.

Marichka, Jean. *La Peste en Afrique septentrionale*. Algiers, 1927.

Périer, Jean. *De l'hygiène en Algérie*. Paris, 1847.

Renaud, P.-J. "Recherches historiques sur les épidémies du Maroc. La peste de 1799." *Hespéris*, 1 (1921), pp. 160-82.

———. "La Peste de 1818 au Maroc." *Hespéris*, 3 (1923), pp. 13-36.

_____. "Un nouveau document marocain sur la peste de 1799." *Hespéris*, 5 (1925), pp. 83-90.

Sebag, Paul. "La Peste dans la Régence de Tunis aux XVIIe et XVIIIe siècles." *IBLA*, No. 109 (1965), pp. 35-48. This article contains all the bibliography relevant to Tunisia on this subject.

SOCIAL STRUCTURES

Bel, Alfred. *La Religion musulmane en Berbérie*. Paris, 1938.

Berque, Jacques. *Etudes d'histoire rurale maghrébine*. Tangiers and Fez, 1938.

_____. *Structures sociales du Haut Atlas*. Paris, 1955.

_____. "Qu'est-ce qu'une tribu nord-africaine?" *Eventail de l'histoire vivante. Mélanges Lucien Febvre*. vol I. (Paris, 1953), pp. 261-71.

Bourdieu, Pierre. *The Algerians*. Boston, 1962.

_____. *Esquisse d'une théorie de la pratique, précédé de trois études d'ethnologie kabyle*. Geneva, 1972.

Bousquet, Georges-Henri. *L'Islam maghrébin*. 2nd edition. Algiers, 1946.

Depont, Octave and Coppolani, Xavier. *Les Confréries religieuses musulmanes*. Algiers, 1897.

Emerit, Marcel. "Au début du XIXe siècle: les tribus privilégiées en Algérie." *Annales ESC* (January-February 1966), pp. 44-58.

Hanoteau, Adolphe and Letourneux, Aristide. *La Kabylie et les coutumes kabyles*. Paris, 1873.

Hart, David. "Segmentary Systems and the Role of 'Five "Fifths"' in Tribal Morocco." *Revue de l'occident musulman et de la Méditerranée*, 1967, pp. 65-95.

Montagne, Robert. *Les Berbères et le Makhzen dans le sud du Maroc. Essai sur la transformation politique des Berbères sédentaires (groupe Chleuh)*. Paris, 1930.

_____. *The Berbers*. London, 1973. This work is an abridgement of Montagne's larger study and contains its most important findings.

Pascon, P. *L'Histoire sociale et les structures agraires de la région du Haouz de Marrakech*. Paris, 1975.

Rinn, Louis. *Marabouts et Khouan*. Algiers, 1884.

Rondot, Pierre. "Assemblées traditionnelles chez les Nefza."

Cahiers de Tunisie, no. 10 (1955), pp. 267-75.

Valensi, Lucette. *Fellahs tunisiens: L'Economie rurale et la vie des campagnes aux XVIIIe et XIXe siècles.* Paris and The Hague, 1977.

THE RURAL ECONOMY

On rural life as a whole, the most important studies are the following regional monographs:

Berque, Jacques. *Etudes d'histoire rurale maghrébine.* Tangiers and Fez, 1938.

Despois, Jean. *La Tunisie orientale. Sahel et basses steppes.* Paris, 1955. A typology of life styles more refined than that which has been presented in this work may be found in Despois' *L'Afrique du Nord.*

Isnard, Hildebert. *La Réorganisation de la propriété rurale dans la Mitidja.* Algiers, 1947.

Michaux-Bellaire, Edouard, and Salmon, Georges. "Les Tribus arabes de la vallée du Lekkous." *Archives Marocaines,* vol. 6, pp. 219-397.

Nouschi, André. *Enquête sur le niveau de vie des populations rurales constantinoises de la conquête jusqu'en 1919.* Paris and Tunis, 1961.

_____. "La Vita rurale in Algeria prima del 1830." *Studi storici,* 4 (1963), pp. 449-78. This is a substantial overall study.

Complementary information concerning technology and agrarian rituals appears in:

Brunhes, Jean. *L'Irrigation, ses conditions géographiques, ses modes et son organisation dans la péninsule ibérique et dans l'Afrique du Nord.* Paris, 1902. Material pertaining to the oases of the Djerid can be found on pp. 485 ff.

Haudricourt, André and Delamarre, Mariel. *L'Homme et la charrue à travers le monde.* Paris, 1954.

Laoust, E. "Noms et cérémonies des feux de joie chez les Berbères du Haut et de l'Anti-Atlas." *Hespéris* (1921), pp. 3-66, 253-316, 387-420.

Marçais, William, and Guiga, T. *Textes arabes de Takrouna.* Paris, 1925. Vol. I, p. 187 presents a complete bibliography on the plow in North Africa.

Collective practices may be studied through the following articles:

Despois, Jean. "Les Greniers fortifiés de l'Afrique du Nord." *Cahiers de Tunisie,* no. 1 (1953), pp. 38-62. This article contains a bibliography dealing with all of the Maghrib.

Montagne, Robert. "Un magasin collectif de l'Anti-Atlas: l'agadir des Ikouna." *Hespéris,* 9 (1929), pp. 145-266.

Also consult the works of Hanoteau and Letourneux and of Masqueray noted above.

The question of land policies engendered countless debates during the colonial period. The *Revue algérienne et tunisienne de législation et de jurisprudence* (beginning in 1885) and the journals which succeeded it contain some of these discussions. The issue of property has not been isolated in this work but, rather, viewed within the context of collective practices. Among the works which provide a relatively clear view of this matter are the article by André Nouschi cited above and:

Poncet, Jean. *La Colonisation et l'agriculture européennes en Tunisie depuis 1881. Etude de géographie historique et économique.* Paris and The Hague, 1962.

Finally, some attempts at defining the mode of production in the precolonial Maghrib have been made in the following works which present hypotheses rather than define interpretations:

Amin, Samir. *La Nation arabe, nationalisme et lutte de classes.* Paris, 1976.

Benachenhou, Abdellatif. *La Formation du sous-développement en Algérie. Essai sur les limites du développement capitaliste.* Algiers, 1976.

Chentouf, Tayeb. "Où en est la discussion sur la mode de production de l'Algérie précoloniale?" *Revue algérienne des sciences juridiques, économiques et politiques* (June 1973).

Djeghloul, Abdelkader. "Essai de définition du mode de production dominant de l'Algérie précoloniale." *Archives Nationales*, 3 (1975), pp. 57-79. This article was reprinted in the French journal *La Pensée* in December, 1975.

Gallissot, René. "Essai de définition du mode de production de l'Algérie pré-coloniale." *Revue algérienne des sciences juridiques*, no. 2 (1968), pp. 385-412.

_____. "L'Algérie pré-coloniale. Classes sociales en système précapitaliste; mise en question du mode de production féodal."*Cahier du centre d'études et de recherches marxistes*, no. 60 (1968).

_____. "Precolonial Algeria." *Economy and Society*, 4 (1975).

_____. *Marxisme et Algérie*. (Textes de Marx-Engels présentés avec la collaboration de G. Badia). Paris, 1976.

_____and Valensi, Lucette. "Le Maghreb pré-colonial: mode de production archaïque ou mode de production féodal?" *La Pensée*, No. 142 (1968), pp. 57-93. Reprinted in *Sur le féodalisme*. Paris, 1971.

THE CITY AND URBAN BUSINESSES

Berque, Jacques. *French North Africa. The Maghrib Between Two World Wars*. New York, 1967.

Boyer, Pierre. *La Vie quotidienne à Alger à la veille de l'intervention*. Paris, 1963.

Braudel, Fernand.*Capitalism and Material Life, 1400-1800*. New York, 1973.

Brunschvig, Robert. "Urbanisme médiéval et droit musulman." *Revue d'études islamiques* (1947), pp. 127-55.

Caillé, Jacques. *La Ville de Rabat jusqu'au protectorat français*. Paris, 1959.

Carette, Ernest. *Du Commerce de l'Algérie avec l'Afrique centrale et les états barbaresques*. Paris, 1844. This work should be viewed as a source.

_____. "La Caravane vers La Mecque, son rôle commercial." *Annuaire des voyages*, 1845.

Emerit, Marcel. "Les Liaisons terrestres entre le Soudan et l'Afrique du Nord au XVIIIe siècle et au début du XIXe siècle."

Travaux de l'Institut de Recherches Sahariennes, 11 (1954), pp. 29-47.

Feraud, Laurent-Charles. "Les Corporations de métiers à Constantine avant la conquête française." *Revue Africaine* 1872, pp. 451-54.

LeTourneau, Roger. *Fès avant la protectorat.* Casablanca, 1949.

_____. *Fes in the Age of the Merinides.* Norman, Oklahoma, 1961.

Marçais, William. "L'Urbanisme musulman." *Actes du 5e Congrès des Sociétés Savantes,* 1908.

_____. "L'Islamisme et la vie urbaine." *Comptes rendus de l'Académie des Inscriptions et Belles Lettres,* 1928, pp. 86-100.

_____. "La Conception des villes de l'Islam." *Revue de la Méditerranée,* 1945.

Massignon, Louis. "Les Corps de métiers et la cité islamique." *Revue internationale de sociologie,* 28 (1920), pp. 473-89.

Nouschi, André. "Constantine à la veille de la conquête française." *Cahiers de Tunisie,* no. 11 (1955), pp. 371-88.

Raymond, André. "Tunisiens et Maghrébins au Caire au XVIIIe siècle." *Cahiers de Tunisie,* nos. 26-27 (1959), pp. 335-71.

Rodinson, Maxime. *Islam and Capitalism.* New York, 1974.

Valensi, Lucette. "Islam et capitalisme: production et commerce des chechias en Tunisie et en France au XVIIIe siècle et XIXe siècle." *Revue d'histoire moderne et contemporaine,* 16 (July-September, 1969), pp. 376-400.

PRIVATEERING

On the issues of privateering and slavery, there are innumerable historical studies. Only the most thought provoking and those which provide the greatest wealth of information have been included here.

On the merchant marine:

Emerit, Marcel. "L'Essai d'une marine marchande barbaresque au XVIIIe siècle." *Cahiers de Tunisie,* no. 11 (1955), pp. 363-70.

Mathiex, Jean. "Sur la marine marchande barbaresque au

XVIIIe siècle." *Annales ESC*, no. 1 (1958), pp. 87-93.

On privateering itself:

Bono, Salvatore. *I corsari barbareschi*. Turin, 1964. This work contains the most complete bibliography.

Coindreau, Roger. *Les Corsaires de Salé*. Paris, 1948.

Davies, G. "Greek Slaves in Tunis in 1823." *English Historical Review*, 34 (1919), pp. 84-89.

Devoulx, Albert. "Le Registre des prises maritimes." *Revue Africaine*, 15 (1871), pp. 70-79, 149-160, 184-201, 285-299, 362-374, 447-457, and 16 (1872), pp. 70-77, 146-156, 233-240, 292-303.

_____. "La Marine de la Régence d'Alger." *Revue Africaine*, no. 77 (1869), pp. 384-420.

Emerit, Marcel. "Les Aventures de Thedenat, esclave et ministre d'un bey d'Afrique (XVIIIe siècle)." *Revue Africaine*, 1948, pp. 143-56.

Fisher, Godfrey. *Barbary Legend. War, Trade, and Piracy in North Africa (1415-1830)*. Oxford, 1957.

Godechot, J. "La Course maltaise le long des côtes barbaresques à la fin du XVIIIe siècle." *Revue Africaine*, 1952, pp. 105-113.

Grandchamp, Pierre. *Documents relatifs aux corsaires tunisiens (2 octobre 1777-4 mai 1824)*. Tunis, 1925.

_____. "Documents concernant la course dans la Régence de Tunis de 1764 à 1769 et de 1783 à 1843." *Cahiers de Tunisie*, nos 19-20 (1957), pp. 269-340.

Mathiex, Jean. "Trafic et prix de l'homme en Méditerranée aux XVIIe et XVIIIe siècles." *Annales ESC*, 1954, pp. 157-64.

Monlaü, Jean. *Les Etats barbaresques*. Paris, 1964.

Riggio, Achille. "Un Censimento di schiavi in Tunisia ottocentesca." *Archivio storico per la Calabria e la Lucania*, 8 (1938), Fasicules III-IV, pp. 333-52.

On this topic also see the article by Lucette Valensi cited above in *Annales ESC*, 1966.

NORTH AFRICAN TRADE
WITH THE MEDITERRANEAN WORLD

No overall study exists on this subject. The Tunisian and Algerian archives show little promise for the development of a profile of North African commerce. Dealings with the Levant do not readily lend themselves to investigation, much less to quantitative study. The archives of Livorno, Malta, Marseille, and Venice do, however, provide abundant details which ought to be systematically brought together. This work has presented a few samples of the results which can be obtained through such archival investigation.

Braudel, Fernand, and Romano, Ruggiero. *Navires et Marchandise à l'entrée du port de Livourne, 1547-1611*. Paris, 1951.

Carrière, C. "Les Entrées de navires dans le port de Marseille pendant la Révolution." *Provence historique* (June 1957), pp. 200-219.

Debbasch, Yvan. *La Nation française en Tunisie (1577-1835)*. Paris, 1957.

Cherif, Muhammad. "Expansion européenne et difficultés tunisiennes." *Annales ESC*, 25 (May-June 1970), pp. 714-45.

Desfeuilles, P. "Scandinaves et Barbaresques à la fin de l'Ancien Régime." *Cahiers de Tunisie*, No. 15 (1956), pp. 327-49.

Emerit, Marcel. "La Situation économique de la Régence en 1830." *Information historique*, November-December 1952.

Guiral, Pierre. *Marseille et l'Algérie (1830-1841)*. Gap, 1957.

Julien, Charles André. "Marseille et la question d'Alger à la veille de la conquête." *Revue Africaine*, 1919, pp. 16-61.

Masson, Paul. *Histoire des établissements et du commerce français dans l'Afrique barbaresque (1590-1793)*. Paris, 1903.

_____. "A la veille d'une conquête, concessions et compagnies d'Afrique (1800-1830)." *Bulletin de géographie historique et descriptive*, 1909, pp. 48-124.

Mathiex, Jean. "La Ravitaillement maghrébin de Malte au XVIIIe siècle." *Cahiers de Tunisie*, no. 6 (1954), pp. 191-202.

Miège, Jean. *Le Maroc et l'Europe (1830-1894)*. Paris, 1961.

Raymond, André. "Tunisiens et Maghrébins au Caire au XVIIIe siècle." *Cahiers de Tunisie*, nos. 26-27 (1959), pp. 335-71.

_____. *Artisans et commerçants au Caire au XVIIIe siècle*. 2 vols. Damascus, 1973 and 1974.

Romano, Ruggiero. *Commerce et prix du blé à Marseille au XVIIIe siècle*. Paris, 1956.

NORTH AFRICAN STATES

Abun Nasr, Jamil. "The Beylicate in 17th Century Tunisia." *International Journal of Middle Eastern Studies*, 6 (1975), pp. 70-93.

Ben Smail, Muhammad and Valensi, Lucette. "Le règne d'Hammuda Pacha dans la chronique d'Ibn Abi Diyaf."*Cahiers de Tunisie*, Nos. 73-74 (1971), pp. 87-108.

Boyer, Pierre. *L'Evolution de l'Algérie médiane*. Paris, 1960.

Brown, L. Carl. *The Tunisia of Ahmad Bey*. Princeton, 1974.

Boyer, Pierre. "Contribution à l'étude de la politique religieuse des Turcs dans la Régence d'Alger, XVIe-XIXe siècles." *Revue de l'Occident musulman et de la Méditerranée*, I (1966), pp. 11-50.

Geertz, Clifford. *Islam Observed, Religious Development in Morocco and Indonesia*. Chicago, 1971.

Grandchamp, Pierre. "Tableau généalogique des Beys husseinites." *Mélanges d'histoire tunisienne, XVIIe-XXe siècles*. Tunis, 1966, pp. 132-33.

LeTourneau, Roger. "Le Maroc sous la règne de Sidi Mohammed ben Abdallah, 1757-1790." *Revue de l'Occident musulman et de la Méditerranée*, I (1966), pp. 113-33.

Raymond, André. "Une liste des Deys de Tunis de 1500 à 1832."*Cahiers de Tunisie*, no. 32 (1960), pp. 129-36.

RELATIONS WITH THE OTTOMAN EMPIRE

The following works touch on contacts with the Muslim world in general:

Kuran, E. "La Lettre du dernier Dey d'Alger au Grand Vizir de l'Empire Ottoman." *Revue Africaine*, 96 (1952), pp. 188-195.

Mantran, Robert. "L'Evolution des relations entre la Tunisie et l'Empire Ottoman du XVIe au XIXe siècle."*Cahiers de Tunisie*, nos. 26-27 (1959), pp. 319-34.

_____. *Inventaire des documents d'archives turcs du Dar El-Bey*. Paris, 1961.

Intellectual contacts between the Middle East and the Maghrib in the 18th century form the center of the excellent article by André Raymond (1959) cited above.

THE QUESTION OF THE EXISTENCE OF "NATIONS"

Demeerseman, André. "Formulation de l'idée de patrie en Tunisie (1837-1872)." *IBLA*, no. 113 (1966), pp. 35-71 and nos. 114-115 (1966), pp. 109-142.

Emerit, Marcel. *L'Algérie à l'époque d'Abd el Kader*. Paris, 1951.

Hermassi, Elbaki. *Leadership and National Development in North Africa*. Berkeley, California, 1972.

Lacheraf, Mostafa. *L'Algérie, nation et société*. Paris, 1965.

Lacoste, Yves; Nouschi, André; and Prenant, André. *L'Algérie, passé et présent*. Paris, 1960.

Laroui, Abdallah. *Les Origines sociales et culturelles du nationalisme marocain entre 1830 et 1912*. Forthcoming.

Leca, J. and Vatin, J. C. *L'Algérie politique, institutions et régime*. Paris, 1975.

Vatin, J. C. *L'Algérie politique, histoire et sociéte*. Paris, 1974.

RELATIONS WITH THE CHRISTIAN POWERS

Arnoulet, F. "Considerations sur la politique internationale des Beys de Tunis." *Actes du 79eCongrès des Sociétés Savantes*. Paris, 1955.

Bussi, Emilio. "Per la storia dei rapporti con le Reggenze barbaresche." *Studi economico-giurdici pubbilicati per cura della Facolta di giurisprudenze del Universita di Cagliari*, 35 (1952). Padua.

Charles-Roux, François. *France et Afrique du Nord avant 1830, les précurseurs de la conquête*. Paris, 1932.

Dupuy, Emile. *Américains et Barbaresques, 1776-1824*. Paris, 1910.

Esquer, Gabriel. *La Prise d'Alger*. 2nd. edition. Paris, 1929.

Irwin, Ray. *The Diplomatic Relations of the United States with the Barbary Powers, 1776-1816*. Chapel Hill, North Carolina 1931.

Miège, Jean. *Le Maroc et l'Europe (1930-1894)*. 4 vols. Paris, 1961.

Riggio, Achille. "Relazioni della Toscana Granducale con le Reggenza di Tunisi (1818-1825)." *Oriente Moderno*, 20 (1940), pp. 93-124.

———. "Tunisi e il regno di Napoli nei primordi del secolo XIX." *Oriente Moderno,* 27 (1947), pp. 1-23.

PROBLEMS OF INTERPRETATION

Gordon, David. *Self-Determination and History in the Third World.* Princeton, 1971.

Laroui, Abdallah. *The History of the Maghrib.* Princeton, 1977.

GLOSSARY

'abd, pl. 'abid
: Slave. In Morocco, the plural of the word referred particularly to the army of freed slaves maintained by the ruler.

amin
: Any person holding a position of trust, but especially a supervisor or foreman responsible for overseeing the work of specialized laborers.

anfaliz
: Council of elders responsible for tribal governance.

'arsh
: Tribe.

'Ashura
: Religious celebration associated with the beginning of a new year.

awlad
: See walad.

babouche
: Backless leather shoes commonly worn throughout the Maghrib.

bait al-mal
: State treasury. In Tunisia, the bait al-mal was also responsible for administering vacant estates.

barrani
: Foreign or alien. By extension, that part of the Maghribi city in which non-Muslims resided.

bey
: Ottoman provincial governor. This title

	was used by the ruling family in Tunisia and by Algerian provincial officials subordinate to the dey.
burnous	Hooded cloak, usually of wool.
chechia	Tightly fitting cylindrical cap, normally dyed red.
couscoussier	Large pot used in the preparation of couscous, a main dish of steamed semolina and meat or vegetables which is widely consumed in the Maghrib.
dar	See douar.
dey	Turkish title used by the ruler of Algiers.
diwan	Sovereign's cabinet or council of advisors.
douar	Plural of dar, house. The douar was a small village, or a collection of houses.
fellah	Peasant or farmer.
firman	Decree or edict issued by the Ottoman ruler, often to confirm or nominate a provincial office holder.
hajj	Pilgrimage to Mecca which all Muslims hope to perform once in their lives. The word is also used as an honorific title appended to the name of one who has made the pilgrimage.
hausch	Farm or large land holding.
hubus	Charitable or religious foundation. Property which remains inalienable and whose revenue is set aside for pious purposes.
jaish	Army. In Morocco, the term is used to identify those tribes which assisted the central government in maintaining order and collecting taxes.

jamaa't	Literally, a community. A collection of several hamlets.
jama'a	Consultative council composed of the elders of the tribe or village.
janissary	Infantry soldier in the Turkish army or the armies of its provincial governors.
kahiya	Administrative officer of a Tunisian governmental subdivision.
khammas	Sharecropper. Khamsa means five, and traditionally the sharecropper received a fifth of the harvest.
khaznadar	Treasurer.
khutba	Sermon delivered at the mosque during the Friday noon service.
leff	Alliance or coalition of a number of tribes, usually very fluid and dissolved or reformed according to circumstances. Also called soff.
madrasa	Religious school approximately of the secondary level, often associated with a mosque.
makhzan	Literally, a storehouse and, by extension, the central government in Morocco.
marabout	Religious figure frequently believed to be endowed with supernatural powers. The word is also used in the Maghrib to denote the tomb or shrine of such an individual.
ma'una	Mutual help or assistance.
métal	French corruption of the Tunisian mathar, a unit of measure equal to roughly twenty liters.
milk	Private property.

mu'allim	Master craftsman.
mufti	Muslim religious figure who delivered formal legal opinions.
muhtasib	Official charged with surveillance of the market place and insuring that no frauds or injustices were perpetrated there.
odjak	Janissary corps.
pasha	Honorific title indicating an individual of rank.
qaddus	Small cup attached to a waterwheel used in traditional irrigation systems.
qadi	Muslim judge.
qaid	Leader or chief. A government officer responsible for the supervision of several tribes.
qaid al-marsa	Official in charge of a port.
qasba	Fortress or citadel. Usually the highest point in the city.
rais	Head or chief. Used in North Africa to refer especially to the privateer captains.
rihla	Travel literature.
riwaq	Space at al-Azhar Mosque University in Cairo which is divided according to its occupants' provenance.
sahel	Coast. The term is used extensively in Tunisia with reference to the fertile eastern Mediterranean coast between Sousse and Sfax.
shabbak	Small, three-masted vessel used in commerce and privateering.
shaikh	Literally, an old and venerable man, but usually referring to a tribal chief.

sharif, pl. ashraf or shurfa	Distinguished or notable person. Especially an individual who can trace his ancestry to the Prophet and, consequently, merits public respect.
shawush	Minor official of the government.
soff	See leff.
sultan	Abstract noun meaning power. By extension, the ruler who exercises temporal power. Title used by the Moroccan sovereign.
suq	Market.
surra	Bag or purse filled with money and used in trade.
tadhkira	Permit. In Tunisia, specifically, an export license.
tell	Hill. Usually used in reference to the hills immediately beyond the coastal plain.
'urf	Customary, or pre-Islamic, law prevalent in Berber regions of the Maghrib.
'ushr	Tithe.
wad'	Votive feast.
wadi	River.
wakil al-kharidj	Minister of foreign affairs.
walad, pl. awlad	Son. In the plural the term was used in the sense of ''the tribe of,'' since tribes were felt to have common ancestors.
zawiya	Building housing the tomb of a marabout and often belonging to a religious brotherhood which used it for meetings.

INDEX

149

THE SURVIVAL OF
ETHIOPIAN INDEPENDENCE
Sven Rubenson

How did it happen that Ethiopia alone of all the great indigenous states of Africa preserve its independence throughout
the long period of European expansion? How did Ethiopia survive the Scramble for Africa?

In this important work, Professor Rubenson, who has lived
and taught for many years in Ethiopia, has tackled this key and
intriguing question by examining the evolution of national
consciousness and foreign policy from the initial contacts with
Britain and France in the early nineteenth century to the famous battle of Adwa in 1896. Throughout he challenges the
commonly held views of the country's history and argues that
Ethiopia's survival was not merely due to its singular geographical features, its isolation from European imperial intrigue
nor feebleness of the Egyptian and Italian armies that attacked
its highland fastnesses. The author's main objective has been
to write a history of Ethiopia from the Ethiopian perspective,
and in doing so he has turned away from traditional European
sources and accompanying biases to base his history wherever
possible on local chronicles and documents. This study is within
the mainstream of modern African historical scholarship where
the emphasis is on African rather than European colonizers.

"A major contribution which eclipses much that has been
written on the subject....The book is attractively produced,
well-written....Professor Rubenson displays a fine command
of European and Ethiopian sources (the introductory survey of
sources is of the greatest value)."
—*Times Literary Supplement*

*437 pp. / maps, illustrations, documents, bibliography, index /
ISBN 0-8419-0374-3 (c); -0375-1 (p)*

 AFRICANA PUBLISHING COMPANY
A division of Holmes & Meier Publishers, Inc.
30 Irving Place, New York, N.Y. 10003